THE FUTURE OF WARFARE

Military Trends and the Future of Warfare

The Changing Global Environment and Its Implications for the U.S. Air Force

FORREST E. MORGAN AND RAPHAEL S. COHEN

 PROJECT AIR FORCE

Prepared for the United States Air Force
Approved for public release; distribution unlimited

For more information on this publication, visit www.rand.org/t/RR2849z3

Library of Congress Cataloging-in-Publication Data is available for this publication.
ISBN: 978-1-9774-0297-4

Published by the RAND Corporation, Santa Monica, Calif.
© Copyright 2020 RAND Corporation
RAND® is a registered trademark.

Cover: RAND photography/Dori Walker
Spine: combo1982/Getty Images, matejmo/Getty Images, StudioM1/Getty Images

Support RAND
Make a tax-deductible charitable contribution at
www.rand.org/giving/contribute

www.rand.org

Preface

Where will the next war occur? Who will fight in it? Why will it occur? How will it be fought? Researchers with RAND Project AIR FORCE's Strategy and Doctrine Program attempted to answer these questions about the future of warfare—specifically, those conflicts that will drive a U.S. and U.S. Air Force response—by examining the key geopolitical, economic, environmental, geographic, legal, informational, and military trends that will shape the contours of conflict between now and 2030. This report on military trends and the future of warfare is one of a series that grew out of this effort. The other reports in the series are

- Raphael S. Cohen et al., *The Future of Warfare in 2030: Project Overview and Conclusions* (RR-2849/1-AF)
- Raphael S. Cohen, Eugeniu Han, and Ashley L. Rhoades, *Geopolitical Trends and the Future of Warfare: The Changing Global Environment and Its Implications for the U.S. Air Force* (RR-2849/2-AF)
- Howard J. Shatz and Nathan Chandler, *Global Economic Trends and the Future of Warfare: The Changing Global Environment and Its Implications for the U.S. Air Force* (RR-2849/4-AF)
- Shira Efron, Kurt Klein, and Raphael S. Cohen, *Environment, Geography, and the Future of Warfare: The Changing Global Environment and Its Implications for the U.S. Air Force* (RR-2849/5-AF)
- Bryan Frederick and Nathan Chandler, *Restraint and the Future of Warfare: The Changing Global Environment and Its Implications for the U.S. Air Force* (RR-2849/6-AF).

This volume examines six military trends by asking four key questions for each trend. First, what does research say about how this variable shapes the conduct of warfare? Second, how has this variable historically shaped the conduct of warfare, especially in the post–Cold War era? Third, how might this variable be expected to change through 2030? And finally, but perhaps most importantly, how might this variable affect the future of warfare in this time frame, especially as it relates to the U.S. armed forces and the U.S. Air Force in particular? By answering these questions, it is hoped that this report will paint a picture of how conventional military capabilities and operations will shape conflict over the next decade and beyond.

This research was sponsored by the Director of Strategy, Concepts and Assessments, Deputy Chief of Staff for Strategic Plans and Requirements (AF/A5S). It is part of a larger study, entitled *The Future of Warfare*, that assists the Air Force in assessing trends in the future strategic environment for the next Air Force strategy. This report should be of value to the national security community and interested members of the general public, especially those with an interest in how global trends will affect the conduct of warfare. Comments are welcome and should be sent to the authors, Forrest E. Morgan and Raphael S. Cohen. Research was completed in October 2018.

RAND Project AIR FORCE

RAND Project AIR FORCE (PAF), a division of the RAND Corporation, is the U.S. Air Force's federally funded research and development center for studies and analyses. PAF provides the Air Force with independent analyses of policy alternatives affecting the development, employment, combat readiness, and support of current and future air, space, and cyber forces. Research is conducted in four programs: Force Modernization and Employment; Manpower, Personnel, and Training; Resource Management; and Strategy and Doctrine. The research reported here was prepared under contract FA7014-16-D-1000.

Additional information about PAF is available on our website: www.rand.org/paf.

This report documents work originally shared with the U.S. Air Force in September 2018. The draft report, issued September 18, 2018, was reviewed by formal peer reviewers and U.S. Air Force subject-matter experts.

Contents

CHAPTER FOUR

CHAPTER FIVE

CHAPTER SIX

Figures and Tables

Figures

Tables

Summary

This report examines some of the most significant factors shaping the future of warfare over the next ten to 15 years: changes in the size, quality, and character of military forces available to the United States and its potential adversaries. In it, we follow sponsor guidance to focus on overarching trends rather than to provide an adversary-by-adversary analysis, and we avoid trends covered in other volumes of this series. Instead, this volume identifies six significant trends that will shape who and where the United States is most likely to fight in the future, how those wars will be conducted, and why they will occur.[1] Table S.1 summarizes findings regarding these trends and the challenges they present.

As the table indicates, the risks of war over the next ten to 15 years will derive largely from perceptions of shifts in regional correlations of force. With U.S. conventional forces reduced in size, China—and, to a lesser extent, Russia—will narrow the qualitative gap and might calculate that the United States lacks sufficient capacity to respond effectively. China and Russia, however, likely will prefer to achieve their objectives "on the cheap"—i.e., with the least cost in international reproach and the lowest risk of provoking military conflict

---

[1] For an overview of the key geopolitical, economic, environmental, geographic, legal, informational, and military trends that will shape the contours of conflict between now and 2030, see the study's summary report. Raphael S. Cohen, Nathan Chandler, Shira Efron, Bryan Frederick, Eugeniu Han, Kurt Klein, Forrest E. Morgan, Ashley L. Rhoades, Howard J. Shatz, and Yuliya Shokh, *The Future of Warfare in 2030: Project Overview and Conclusions*, Santa Monica, Calif.: RAND Corporation, RR-2849/1-AF, 2020.

Table S.1
Summary of Findings

Trend	Who Will Fight	How the United States Will Fight	Where the United States Will Fight	Why the United States Will Fight
Decreasing U.S. conventional force size		Multidomain under nuclear shadow with some amount of artificial intelligence (AI)		Regional aggressor calculates that the United States lacks capacity to respond effectively in a given theater because of its other global commitments
Increasing modernization and professionalization of near-peer forces	China or Russia vs. United States and select allies or partners	Multidomain under nuclear shadow with some amount of AI	East China Sea, Taiwan, South China Sea, Baltics, or elsewhere on peripheries	China or Russia calculates that it can deny the United States sufficient access to defeat effort to change territorial status quo
Development of asymmetric strategies by second-tier powers	Iran or North Korea vs. United States, allies, and partners	Neutralize selective capabilities, then destroy large but less-sophisticated forces	Middle East or Korean peninsula	Iranian machinations/North Korean provocations lead to war
Potential adversaries' increasing use of "gray zone" tactics	Quasi-military or covert state forces, nonstate actors	Subconventional or hybrid, potentially escalating to conventional	In disputed territories and areas where state control is weak	States victimized by covert or proxy forces will need support
Weakening of the state's monopoly on violence	Heavily armed individuals and groups	Subconventional or hybrid	Areas of failed or weak state control—Africa, Middle East, South Asia	States unable to restrain heavily armed individuals and groups will need support
AI as a class of potentially disruptive technologies	Highly advanced states	Multidomain under nuclear shadow with autonomous weapons		Regional aggressor believes its AI capabilities are sufficient to change the status quo

with the United States. Instead, both likely will ramp up their use of *gray-zone tactics*—employing incremental aggression, information warfare, proxy forces, and covert special operations forces to obtain their regional objectives but staying below the U.S. threshold of conventional response.

Iran and North Korea do not have—and are unlikely to develop—capabilities to match those of the United States and its regional allies. Consequently, these nations are developing selected asymmetric capabilities to deter U.S. intervention and developing gray-zone strategies for obtaining their aggressive objectives. If such strategies ultimately lead to war, U.S. forces will need to find ways to neutralize these asymmetric capabilities and destroy substantial portions of those adversaries' large but less-sophisticated forces.

The use of substate actors as proxy fighters in these strategies will continue a long-term trend of weakening the state's monopoly on violence in many areas of the world. As aggressive states arm individuals and groups in regions they seek to destabilize or annex, weaker states will have difficulty containing the resulting violence and likely will turn to the United States for support.

Developments in military applications of AI might help U.S. forces obtain objectives in both conventional and unconventional operations, thereby mitigating some of these trends. However, these capabilities come with serious risks that will need to be managed, and the United States will not have a monopoly on access to them. U.S. leaders will need to find ways to maximize the benefits they offer while mitigating their inevitable risks.

Acknowledgments

This study would not have been possible without the help of several key people. First and foremost, we would like to thank Brig Gen David Hicks, Col Linc Bonner, and Scott Wheeler of the Air Force A5S for sponsoring this project and guiding it along the way. We would also like to thank Paula Thornhill, the Project AIR FORCE strategy doctrine program director, for her guidance and mentorship of this study. We also thank Stephen Watts and Giselle Donnelly for their thoughtful reviews of an earlier draft of this work.

Abbreviations

A2/AD	anti-access/area-denial
AI	artificial intelligence
ASBM	anti-ship ballistic missile
ASCM	anti-ship cruise missile
CR	continuing resolution
DMZ	demilitarized zone
DoD	U.S. Department of Defense
FY	fiscal year
IADS	integrated air defense systems
IISS	International Institute for Strategic Studies
IRBM	intermediate-range ballistic missile
IRGC	Islamic Revolutionary Guard Corps
ISR	intelligence, surveillance, and reconnaissance
MRBM	medium-range ballistic missile
NATO	North Atlantic Treaty Organization
NCO	noncommissioned officer
OCO	overseas contingency operations
PLA	People's Liberation Army
RDT&E	research, development, testing, and evaluation
SAM	surface-to-air missile
SRBM	short-range ballistic missile

TOA	total obligation authority
UAV	unmanned aerial vehicle
USAF	U.S. Air Force

CHAPTER ONE

Military Trends

The 2018 *National Defense Strategy* proclaims that the Department of Defense (DoD) is at a critical juncture. It argues that "we are emerging from a period of strategic atrophy, aware that our competitive military advantage has been eroding," and that "inter-state strategic competition, not terrorism, is now the primary concern in U.S. national security."[1] Neither statement, however, is self-evident. How has the U.S. "competitive military advantage" eroded? And what exactly does it mean in a practical sense for DoD to be focused on "inter-state strategic competition" going forward? This report answers these questions by examining projected changes in the size, quality, and character of military forces available to the United States and its potential adversaries over the next ten to 15 years and exploring how these shifts, in turn, could affect the future of warfare.

After briefly outlining the methodology used in this analysis, we identify six significant trends. The first is the diminishing size of U.S. conventional military forces that has occurred throughout the post–Cold War era. This phenomenon is particularly worrisome in juxtaposition with the second and third trends, which are the increasing modernization and professionalization of the military forces of near-peer competitors and the fact that second-tier powers are focusing on selective asymmetric capabilities to offset superior U.S. and allied forces. The fourth trend we examine is how potential opponents are using gray-zone tactics, such as proxy groups and covert military forces, to

---

[1] DoD, *Summary of the 2018 National Defense Strategy of the United States of America: Sharpening the American Military's Competitive Edge,* Washington, D.C., 2018, p. 1.

obtain objectives while staying below the threshold of U.S. military response. This contributes to a fifth trend, a weakening of the state's monopoly on violence. Finally, we consider a sixth trend, one that could change much about how wars are fought in the future: the rise of artificial intelligence (AI) and related advances in military technology. Taken together, these trends suggest the true meaning of an "eroding" competitive military advantage: The real danger for the joint force is not that it will be replaced in 2030 as the world's dominant military actor but that it will be spread so thin across regions, adversaries, and threats that it will lose its dominant position in any single type of conflict. This risk of defeat-by-piecemeal is, perhaps, particularly acute for the U.S. Air Force (USAF) because air, space, and cyber power will likely play crucial roles regardless of the region, adversary, or type of conflict with which the United States might engage in the future.

With an almost infinite number of possible trends that could shape the future of warfare and only a finite amount of space for this report, we applied three limiting factors to select the trends on which we focus. First, at the sponsors' request, we avoided a strictly adversary-based analysis—looking at China, Russia, Iran, North Korea, and terrorist groups individually. Instead, we focused on broader, crosscutting trends.[2] Second, we tried to avoid overlap between the trends covered here and those covered in the other volumes in this series. Most notably, trends about where and why states have used force in the past and will likely do in the future are covered in *Geopolitical Trends and the Future of Warfare,* and trends about the resources that states will have at their disposal—including questions about the defense industrial base—are covered in *Global Economic Trends and the Future of Warfare.*[3] By contrast, this report focuses more narrowly on trends about military capac-

---

[2]   DoD, 2018, p. 1.

[3]   Raphael S. Cohen, Eugeniu Han, and Ashley L. Rhoades, *Geopolitical Trends and the Future of Warfare: The Changing Global Environment and Its Implications for the U.S. Air Force,* Santa Monica, Calif.: RAND Corporation, RR-2849/2, 2020; Howard J. Shatz and Nathan Chandler, *Global Economic Trends and the Future of Warfare: The Changing Global Environment and Its Implications for the U.S. Air Force,* Santa Monica, Calif.: RAND Corporation, RR-2849/4, 2020.

ity, capability, and likely methods of employment. Potential posture changes, however, are examined in the *Geopolitical Trends* report.

The six trends discussed here still do not represent a comprehensive list of all the military trends that could affect the future of warfare. For example, we discuss U.S. and adversary military trends but largely exclude allied military trends.[4] Similarly, we focus on the implications of certain game-changing technologies (such as AI), but there are other technologies (such as directed energy and biotechnology) that arguably could have been added to the list. We chose to examine AI because it is a broad class of technologies that, collectively, could change the character of war in the coming decades.[5] Admittedly, these choices came down to a judgment call and they do pose limitations to this work. Nonetheless, each of the trends chosen will profoundly shape the future of warfare.

---

[4] Allied contributions are discussed at length in Cohen, Han, and Rhoades, 2020, and to a lesser extent in Shatz and Chandler, 2020.

[5] For example, the *National Defense Strategy* calls out advanced computing, "big data" analytics, AI, autonomy, robotics, directed energy, hypersonics, and biotechnology as potentially significant areas for the future of warfare. Although AI is specifically named, four of the other seven areas also fall into the class of technologies generally described as AI. DoD, 2018, p. 3.

CHAPTER TWO

Trend 1: Decreasing U.S. Conventional Force Size

One of the most direct ways of measuring a state's military power is to consider the size of its conventional forces. By this simplistic metric, the United States is visibly less powerful than it was at the end of the Cold War and could grow even weaker in the future. Of course, decreases in the size of U.S. forces are partially offset by improved military quality during the same period because advances in technology have made each U.S. force element considerably more lethal than it was a quarter of a century ago. However, "quantity has a quality all its own," as an oft-repeated adage goes. No matter how capable a state's military forces are, smaller numbers cannot provide the degree of presence across multiple regions that larger numbers can. The composition of a state's military forces is also important; as we demonstrate in this chapter, U.S. forces have shifted in composition in ways that could leave them less prepared for emerging challenges in the coming ten to 15 years.

Context: Size of Military Forces Affects Probability of War and Chances of Victory

Classical military theory and a substantial body of empirical research suggest that military force size affects not only the likelihood of war, but also the chances of victory. Prussian military theorist Carl von Clausewitz emphasized that in tactics and strategy, "superiority of numbers is the most common element in victory."[1] Having superior numbers does not guarantee victory in war, by any means, but "the first rule [in strategy] should be: put the largest possible army into the field."[2] Similarly, Swiss theorist Antoine Henri de Jomini argued that one great principle underlies all operations in war: "To throw by strategic movements the mass of an army, successively, upon the decisive points of a theater of war, and also upon the enemy's communications, without compromising one's own."[3]

Sensing this truism, potential adversaries have generally avoided war when confronted with superior military forces. In 1983, John Mearsheimer demonstrated that reliably deterring an aggressive conventional adversary requires posturing sufficient forces to convince the opponent that the attack would be defeated—or at least defended against effectively enough that the opponent risks getting bogged down in a costly war of attrition.[4] The following year, Paul Huth and Bruce Russett found the defender's local military superiority to be one of the principal determinants of deterrence success.[5] A substantial body of work has been done in subsequent years supporting these findings.[6]

---

[1]   Carl von Clausewitz, *On War*, ed. and trans., Michael Howard and Peter Paret, Princeton, N.J.: Princeton University Press, 1976, p. 194.

[2]   Von Clausewitz, 1976, p. 195.

[3]   Antoine Henri de Jomini, *The Art of War: A New Edition with Appendices and Maps*, trans. G. H. Mendell and W. P. Craighill, Philadelphia, Pa.: J. B. Lippincott & Co., 1862, reprint in Westport, Conn.: Greenwood Press, undated, p. 63.

[4]   John J. Mearsheimer, *Conventional Deterrence*, Ithaca, N.Y.: Cornell University Press, 1983.

[5]   Paul Huth and Bruce Russett, "What Makes Deterrence Work? Cases from 1900 to 1980," *World Politics*, Vol. 36, No. 4, 1984.

[6]   See for instance: Edward Rhodes, Conventional Deterrence," *Comparative Strategy*, Vol. 19, No. 3, 2000; Karen Ruth Adams, "Attack and Conquer? International Anarchy and the Offense-Defense-Deterrence Balance," *International Security*, Vol. 28, No. 3, Winter 2003–2004; Michael Petersen, "The Perils of Conventional Deterrence by Punishment," *War on the Rocks*, November 11, 2006; and Michael S. Gerson, "Conventional Deterrence in the Second Nuclear Age," *Parameters*, Vol. 39, No. 3, Autumn 2009.

Historical Trend: U.S. Military Forces Have Gotten Smaller, and Their Composition and Posture Have Shifted

After the end of the Cold War, the U.S. military shrank dramatically. One of the most visible signs of these reductions in capacity is the total number of U.S. active-duty military personnel (see Figure 2.1). With the demise of the Soviet Union and no credible state threat on the horizon, U.S. leaders and the public alike were eager to draw down excess military forces and enjoy the "peace dividend" expected from reduced military spending.[7]

As Figure 2.1 also indicates, the drawdown was curtailed following the terrorist attacks of September 11, 2001, when the United States began putting more people in uniform to fight the wars in Afghanistan and the Middle East. However, the decline in military manpower resumed as the United States completed the withdrawal of most of its troops from Iraq in 2011 and began withdrawing from Afghanistan in 2012. That slide bottomed out in 2017, when Donald Trump's presidential administration began increasing end strength in 2018.

As important as the overall numbers, however, is where these troops have been located. At the end of the Cold War, the United States drew down its overseas presence, especially in Europe and, to a lesser extent, in Asia. Without the Soviet Union, Europe seemingly faced little conventional threat and disbanding units from overseas was an easier political hurdle than closing bases in the United States and taking jobs out of congressional districts. After the start of the Global War on Terrorism, overseas presence went back up, especially in the Middle East. After Russia's invasion of Crimea in 2014, the United States began returning forces to Europe. Nonetheless, as depicted in Figure 2.2, U.S. military presence overseas has hit a 60-year low.[8]

Another important consideration is that U.S. military forces have shifted in composition. Troops were formerly organized, trained, and

---

[7] See, for instance, Richard Nixon, "Save the Peace Dividend," *New York Times*, November 19, 1992.

[8] Stacie L. Pettyjohn, *U.S. Global Defense Posture, 1783–2011*, Santa Monica, Calif.: RAND Corporation, MG-1244-AF, 2011; Kristen Bialik, "U.S. Active-Duty Military Presence Overseas Is at Its Smallest in Decades," Pew Research Center, August 22, 2017.

Figure 2.1
Total U.S. Active Duty Military Personnel, 1990–2018

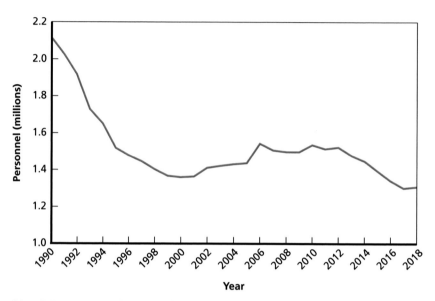

SOURCES: International Institute for Strategic Studies (IISS), "The United States," *The Military Balance*, Vols. 90–103, 1990–2003; IISS, "North America," *The Military Balance*, Vols. 104–118, 2004–2018.
NOTE: Includes uniformed personnel in the four DoD military services but not personnel in the U.S. Coast Guard.

equipped to conduct high-speed maneuver warfare against heavily armored conventional adversaries, such as the Soviet Union; the focus has changed in recent years to a force trained to conduct counterinsurgency and counterterrorism operations against substate adversaries. Figure 2.3 reflects this shift in emphasis.[9]

This figure shows the numbers of select major combat systems in service from 1990 to 2017 and the declines in the kinds of weapon systems needed to fight near-peer conventional state adversaries. The

---

[9]   By showing force and spending levels from 1990 to 2017, we do not mean to imply that force levels at the end of the Cold War are a benchmark against which today's capabilities should be measured. The points we are making are simply that overall force levels have declined and the composition of available forces has shifted, making fewer conventional capabilities available.

Figure 2.2
Total U.S. Active Duty Personnel Overseas

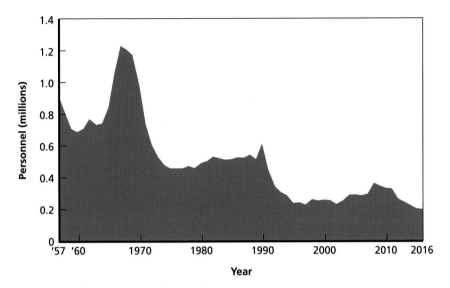

SOURCE: Bialik, 2017. Used with permission.
NOTES: Estimates are as of September 30 in each year. Numbers of personnel represent U.S. active-duty Army, Navy, Marine Corps, and USAF troops overseas. They exclude the U.S. Coast Guard, National Guard, reserve and civilian personnel, as well as troops in the United States and its territories.

Navy's inventory of ships has been reduced by slightly more than half since 1990; likewise, the USAF has less than half the number of manned combat aircraft it had at the end of the Cold War. Most significantly, the Army's inventory of main battle tanks is only 15 percent of what it was in 1990.[10] Again, much of this reduction in forces can be attributed to the post–Cold War drawdown in the 1990s, but it should be noted that tanks and manned combat aircraft were further reduced starting in the late 2000s when the services began tailoring their forces to fight substate adversaries more effectively. During the same period,

---

[10] The USAF is not the only service that has manned combat aircraft. The U.S. Marine Corps also has some main battle tanks. Nevertheless, the USAF's inventory of manned, fixed-wing aircraft is far larger than that of the other services, and the Army is the principal repository of main battle tanks. The cuts shown are largely representative of the force structure writ large.

Figure 2.3
Select U.S. Major Combat Systems, 1990–2017

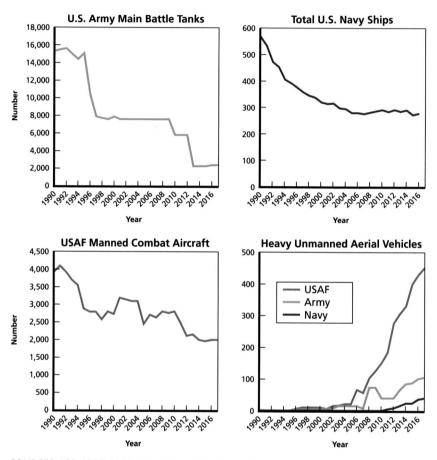

SOURCES: IISS, 1990–2003; IISS, 2004–2018; Naval History and Heritage Command, "U.S. Navy Active Ship Force Levels, 2000–2006," November 17, 2017.

the USAF, Army, and Navy inventories of heavy unmanned aerial vehicles (UAVs) climbed dramatically.[11] These systems are ideal for

---

[11] Heavy UAVs are those large enough that runways are required for them to take off and land. The Army, Navy, and Marine Corps also operate hundreds of medium UAVs, which can be launched from ships or trucks, and even larger numbers of light UAVs, which are small enough to be launched by hand.

long-loiter intelligence, surveillance, and reconnaissance (ISR) operations in uncontested airspace and conducting strikes against high-value targets, such as terrorist leaders, but they would have considerably less utility in conventional operations against near-peer adversaries, where advanced integrated air-defense systems (IADS) would challenge their survivability.

Importantly, this shift in size, posture, and composition of the U.S. military was not accompanied by corresponding reductions in U.S. military commitments. To the contrary, some U.S. alliances—such as the North Atlantic Treaty Organization—expanded during the post–Cold War period, and the frequency of U.S. use of military force increased after the Cold War period.[12] Somewhat quixotically, at least judging from formal DoD strategies, the requirements on the joint force have increased while its capacity to fulfill these requirements has declined.[13]

The net result is that the U.S. military faces a means-ends mismatch. It remains the strongest force in the world, but U.S. ability to gain and maintain local military supremacy—especially against its most formidable competitors, China and Russia—has declined.[14]

---

[12] See Nuno P. Monteiro, "Rest Unassured: Why Unipolarity Has Not Been Peaceful," *International Security*, Vol. 36, No. 3, Winter 2011–2012.

[13] See Raphael S. Cohen, *The History and Politics of Defense Reviews*, Santa Monica, Calif.: RAND Corporation, RR-2278-AF, 2018, pp. 48–50.

[14] For example, see Eric Heginbotham, Michael Nixon, Forrest E. Morgan, Jacob L. Heim, Jeff Hagen, Sheng Li, Jeffrey Engstrom, Martin C. Libicki, Paul DeLuca, David A. Shlapak, David R. Frelinger, Burgess Laird, Kyle Brady, and Lyle J. Morris, *The U.S.-China Military Scorecard: Forces, Geography, and the Evolving Balance of Power, 1996–2017*, Santa Monica, Calif.: RAND Corporation, RR-392-AF, 2015; David A. Shlapak and Michael Johnson, *Reinforcing Deterrence on NATO's Eastern Flank: Wargaming the Defense of the Baltics*, Santa Monica, Calif.: RAND Corporation, RR-1253-A, 2016; David Ochmanek, Peter A. Wilson, Brenna Allen, John Speed Myers, and Carter C. Price, *U.S. Military Capabilities and Forces for a Dangerous World: Rethinking the U.S. Approach to Force Planning*, Santa Monica, Calif.: RAND Corporation, RR-1782-1-RC, 2017.

Future Projection: It Will Be Difficult to Reverse This Trend in the Next Ten to 15 Years

DoD has recognized this trend and plans to reverse it. Stating that "great power competition is now the primary focus," DoD's fiscal year (FY) 2019 budget request petitions Congress for $74 billion over that provided in the FY 2018 continuing resolution (CR), which would amount to 10-percent real growth in defense spending.[15] If this request is met, funding for procurement will increase 13 percent, allowing the services to purchase additional units of several major weapon systems. DoD plans to use the money in FY 2019 to add ten more F/A-18E/F fighter aircraft, three more P-8A antisubmarine warfare aircraft, an additional *Arleigh Burke*–class destroyer, and fleet oilers.[16] The funding increase will also allow for substantial increases in munitions, such as joint direct attack munitions, guided multiple launch rocket systems, small diameter bomb IIs, and joint air-to-ground missiles—all capabilities that would be important in a conflict with a near-peer competitor. In addition, DoD is requesting a 22.8-percent increase in funding for research, development, testing, and evaluation (RDT&E).[17] As Figure 2.4 illustrates, if this funding is approved, it will set DoD on a path to restoring what the department maintains are $400 billion of capabilities lost as a result of budget caps since 2011.

With multiple competing domestic spending priorities and a burgeoning budget deficit, getting congressional approval for this spending increase and then sustaining political support for higher defense budgets over the long term is by no means a foregone conclusion. On the other hand, a broader examination of DoD spending in the post–Cold War era indicates that spending cuts in the past five years have not been as draconian as Figure 2.4 seems to suggest. Figure 2.5 shows

---

[15] Office of the Undersecretary of Defense (Comptroller)/Chief Financial Officer, *Defense Budget Overview: United States Department of Defense Fiscal Year 2019 Budget Request*, Washington, D.C.: U.S. Department of Defense, February 2018a, p. 1-2.

[16] Office of the Undersecretary of Defense (Comptroller)/Chief Financial Officer, 2018a, p. 3-3.

[17] Office of the Undersecretary of Defense (Comptroller)/Chief Financial Officer, 2018b.

DoD's total obligation authority (TOA) in each category of spending identified in public law from 1990 to 2018. This figure reflects all DoD expenditures made during that period: base budget authorizations, enacted war and supplemental funding, overseas contingency operations (OCO), emergency funding per Division B of Public Law 115-96,[18] and the FY 2018 CR. All amounts are shown in FY 2019 constant dollars.

As Figure 2.5 indicates, defense spending was cut significantly in the 1990s following the end of the Cold War. However, comparing the

Figure 2.4
Illustration of How the Requested FY 2019 Budget Will Put DoD on the Path to Recovering Lost Capabilities Resulting from Previous Budget Caps

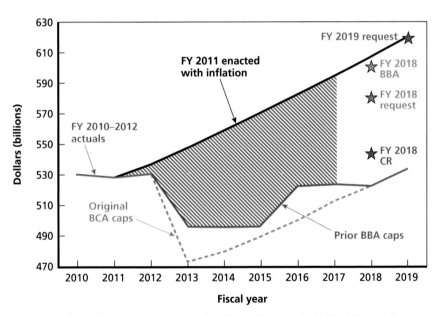

SOURCE: Office of the Undersecretary of Defense (Comptroller)/ Chief Financial Officer, *Fiscal Year 2019 Budget Request*, Washington, D.C.: U.S. Department of Defense, February 2018b.
NOTES: FY 2018 CR = $529B + $15B of OCO-for-base requirements; BCA = Budget Control Act; BBA = Bipartisan Budget Acts (2011, 2013, and 2018).

---

[18] Public Law 115-96, Third Continuing Appropriations for Fiscal Year 2018, Division B, Missile Defense, Title I, Missile Defeat and Defense Enhancements, December 22, 2017.

Figure 2.5
DoD Total Obligation Authority by Public Law, 1990–2018

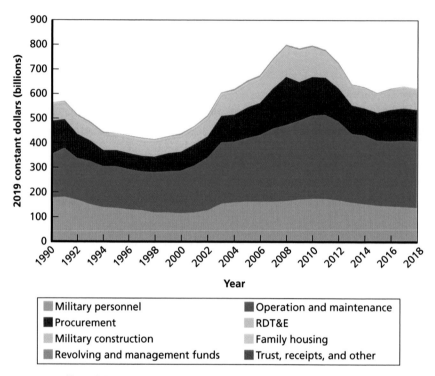

SOURCE: Office of the Undersecretary of Defense (Comptroller)/Chief Financial Officer, *National Defense Budget Estimates for FY 2019*, Washington, D.C.: U.S. Department of Defense, April 2018c, Table 6-1.

TOA in 2018 with that of 1990 reveals that defense spending in the current era is actually higher than it was at the end of the Cold War. This is largely because of OCO spending for ongoing conflicts abroad—the hump from 2003 to 2013, when U.S. involvement in Afghanistan and Iraq was at its greatest, confirms this—but even between 2013 and 2017, when budget caps were in effect, defense spending was higher than it was in 1990. The problem, therefore, is not the amount of money being spent; the problem is what the money is being spent on. As Figure 2.5 shows, a significant majority of defense TOA is spent on military personnel and on operation and maintenance. Conversely, procurement and RDT&E (the categories of spending most needed to restore conventional warfighting capabilities and prepare the force for future wars) receive smaller percentages of the budget.

Personnel and operation and maintenance are necessary and inescapable burdens, but given DoD's request for a substantial increase in spending in FY 2019 to restore capabilities and better prepare for great-power competition, it is instructive to examine how DoD plans to allocate its budget in the out years. Figure 2.6 depicts DoD's projected TOA from 2018 to 2023 and illustrates the effects on spending for procurement, RDT&E, and real total growth if Congress approves the funding as requested.

The sand chart on the left side of Figure 2.6 shows a rise in FY 2019 that reflects the requested funding increase; the bar chart on the right confirms that a significant amount of this money is tagged for procurement and RDT&E—increases of 13 percent and 21.8 percent of TOA, respectively—contributing to the 10-percent increase in real total growth mentioned earlier. However, this is followed by a projected decrease in spending on procurement and RDT&E of 10.4 percent and 4.5 percent, respectively, in 2020, with real total growth declining to 0.2 percent. For the next two years, procurement and RDT&E spending remain relatively stable, with a 4.0-percent bump in procurement, largely offset by a 4.0-percent cut in RDT&E, projected for 2023. Over these years, real total growth is projected to decline to –0.3 percent in 2021 and 2022 and to –0.2 percent in 2023. As the sand chart indicates, DoD projects spending on the main categories authorized by public law to remain at essentially 2018 levels from 2020 to 2023 and expects to rely on OCO and out-year placeholders for OCO to bring the total up to the 2019 level.

All of this suggests that it will be difficult to restore conventional warfighting capabilities lost in the post–Cold War era, even if Congress approves DoD budget requests through 2023. The majority of the defense budget is devoted to supporting military personnel and operations and maintenance, areas in which costs are relatively stable. Costs would decline somewhat if the United States were to end or reduce its involvement in overseas contingencies, but costs would probably need to increase for DoD to add conventional forces. DoD projections for budgets beyond FY 2019 do not reflect substantial increases in funding

Figure 2.6
DoD Projected Total Obligation Authority and Changes in Spending for Procurement and RDT&E and Real Total Growth, 2018–2023

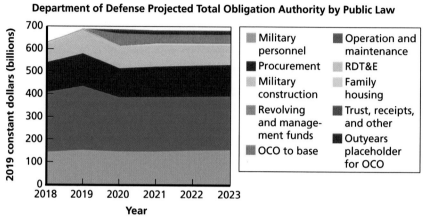

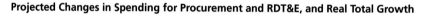

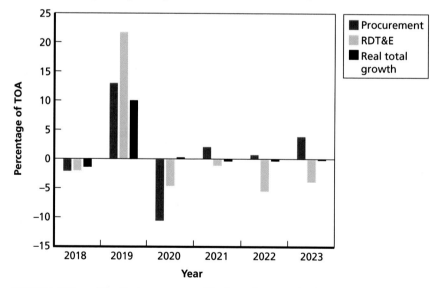

SOURCE: Office of the Undersecretary of Defense (Comptroller)/Chief Financial Officer, 2018c, Table 6-1.

for procurement and RDT&E, the essential areas for restoring conventional warfighting capabilities and preparing for future challenges. It will take persistence and political will to develop and maintain a spending program that provides the capabilities that might be needed in the coming ten to 15 years.[19]

Implications for the U.S. Air Force and the Future of Warfare

With fewer conventional capabilities available, U.S. forces are stretched thinner across regions in which the United States has important interests than they were during the Cold War. Today, the United States faces five principal competitors—China, Russia, Iran, North Korea, and terrorist groups—all simultaneously challenging the United States in different parts of the globe.[20] Unless the United States proves more willing to reduce the number of troops based in the United States—with all the political and economic effects that decision entails—and base them overseas, fewer forces means less of an ability to posture forces forward to deny fait accompli and less capacity to surge in times

---

[19] Although we suggest that the trend of declining U.S. conventional force capacity needs to be reversed, we do not attempt an assessment of how many conventional forces are needed to meet demands over the next ten to 15 years. Such an analysis would require an estimate of what conflicts might occur during that period and what numbers and kinds of forces would be needed to deter or defeat prospective adversaries in those conflicts. For a top-level assessment of possible conflicts over the next ten to 15 years, see Cohen, Han, and Rhoades, 2020. For an analysis of what forces would be needed in conflicts against China, Iran, North Korea, Russia, and Salafist groups, see Ochmanek et al., 2017.

[20] White House, *National Security Strategy of the United States of America*, Washington, D.C., December 2017, p. 25.

of crisis.[21] If the United States ever needs to fight two wars simultaneously, it could face significant capacity constraints.[22]

Understanding this, potential state adversaries might be emboldened to act aggressively at the expense of U.S. and allied interests, if those adversaries believe that the United States lacks either the will or the capacity to respond in a timely fashion.[23] Moreover, without significant forward presence already in theater, USAF, as the nation's military service most able to generate forces quickly, could be called on more frequently to respond to regional conflicts.

Some of the declines in capacity and forward presence can be partially offset by improvements in capability—but only to a certain extent. First, U.S. defense strategy prioritizes forward posture as central to deterring adversaries and reassuring allies.[24] Second, as we shall see in the next chapter, U.S. adversaries—particularly China and Russia—are already catching up to the United States in certain key

---

[21] For the impact of removing Army troops from congressional districts, see Christopher M. Schnaubelt, Craig A. Bond, Frank Camm, Joshua Klimas, Beth E. Lachman, Laurie L. McDonald, Judith D. Mele, Paul Ng, Meagan L. Smith, Cole Sutera, and Christopher Skeels, *The Army's Local Economic Effects*, Santa Monica, Calif.: RAND Corporation, RR-1119-A, 2015.

[22] The current *National Defense Strategy* recommends something less than a full two-war strategy ("defeating aggression by a major power; deterring opportunistic aggression elsewhere") but the bipartisan congressionally appointed National Defense Strategy Commission concluded, "A two-war force sizing construct makes more strategic sense today than at any previous point in the post-Cold War era." Eric Edelman and Gary Roughead, *Providing for the Common Defense: The Assessment and Recommendations of the National Defense Strategy Commission*, Washington, D.C.: U.S. Institute of Peace, 2018, p. 66.

[23] There is an argument that U.S. forward presence could provoke U.S. adversaries and actually increase the chances of conflict, short of war. Statistical analyses of historical cases, for example, show that increased forward presence generally decreases interstate conflict but increases the chances of militarized disputes. (See Angela O'Mahony, Miranda Priebe, Bryan Frederick, Jennifer Kavanagh, Matthew Lane, Trevor Johnston, Thomas S. Szayna, Jakub P. Hlávka, Stephen Watts, and Matthew Povlock, *U.S. Presence and the Incidence of Conflict*, Santa Monica, Calif.: RAND Corporation, RR-1906-A, 2018.) That said, if Russia's actions in Ukraine or China's actions in the South China Sea are driven by motivations other than a negative reaction to U.S. forward presence, the greater chances of deterrence might be worth the added risk of provocation.

[24] DoD, 2018, p. 5; Edelman and Roughead, 2018, p. 33.

areas—and, as we shall see in Chapter Seven, this gap could narrow even further with advances in future technologies, particularly in AI. Should that occur, fewer forces means less margin for error in calculations of superior quality relative to enemy capabilities. Perhaps, this is why the bipartisan congressionally appointed National Defense Strategy Commission concluded, "The United States needs a larger force than it has today if it is to meet the objectives of the strategy. The Army, Navy, and USAF will all need capacity enhancements in addition to—not in place of—the capability and posture changes this Commission recommends."[25]

---

[25] Edelman and Roughead, 2018, p. 66.

CHAPTER THREE

Trend 2: Increasing Modernization and Professionalization of Near-Peer Forces

Context: China and Russia Have Modernized Forces

The United States has long relied on the technological superiority and higher standard of training and professionalization to offset numerical inferiority. Relying on these advantages, U.S. forces, armed with "transformational" capabilities—such as stealth technology, precision-guided weapons, force-enhancement support from space, and systems networking—defeated Iraq and Serbia so handily that former near-peer competitors China and Russia were prompted to begin reforming their antiquated and poorly trained forces. These efforts took considerable time to bear fruit, particularly in Russia, but they have finally begun to manifest and could have serious implications for USAF in the next ten to 15 years.

Historical Trend: China Has Advanced Capabilities; Russia Has Streamlined Military Forces

China's Modern Force Has Advanced Area-Denial and Force-Projection Capabilities

Over most of its history, the People's Republic of China has relied on a military establishment built around a massive army featuring light infantry forces. As late as the mid-1990s, the People's Liberation Army (PLA) consisted of approximately 2.9 million soldiers, most of them poorly trained and operating Chinese versions of early Cold War–era Soviet equipment. China's navy and air force were similarly limited in capability, with submarines and aircraft based on 1950s-vintage Soviet designs.[1] With almost no ability to conduct operations much beyond its borders, China relied on a military doctrine called "Limited Local War," employing massed infantry to overwhelm enemy invaders.[2]

This began to change in the mid-1990s. Shocked by the capabilities that U.S. forces exhibited in the first Gulf War, Chinese leaders concluded that their existing military capabilities and doctrine would not enable the PLA to stand up to U.S. forces should war with the United States occur. Subsequently, Chinese military analysts worked out a plan to develop force projection capabilities patterned after U.S. strengths and anti-access/area-denial (A2/AD) capabilities designed to exploit U.S. vulnerabilities resulting from the geographical challenges of having to operate in the vast Western Pacific region. This concept emerged as an evolving doctrine called "Local Wars Under Informationized Conditions."[3]

The new approach "emphasized the modernization of equipment and improvement of personnel recruitment, training and preparation."[4] The A2/AD aspect of the new doctrine focused on denying U.S. forces the ability to project airpower from land bases and naval platforms in the region and to operate in the airspace around China. China developed a growing arsenal of precision-guided cruise missiles and conventional short-, medium-, and intermediate-range ballistic missiles (SRBMs, MRBMs, and IRBMs); air-, ground-, and sea-launched anti-ship cruise missiles (ASCMs); and the world's first anti-ship ballistic missile (ASBM). Area-denial missions are accomplished mainly via dense and highly sophisticated IADS.[5]

China also developed capabilities to project force into the contested regions it claims in the East China Sea, South China Sea, and

---

[1]   Heginbotham et al., 2015, pp. 26–27.

[2]   Monika Chansoria, "China's Military Doctrine and Strategy: Continuity with Change," *CLAWS Journal*, winter 2009, pp. 100–106.

[3]   Chansoria, 2009, pp. 106–107; Heginbotham et al., 2015, p. 272.

[4]   Heginbotham et al., 2015, p. 28.

[5]   Heginbotham et al., 2015, p. 28.

Taiwan. These capabilities feature at least 37 modern diesel attack submarines, two nuclear attack submarines, and a growing number of new surface vessels, including eight modern destroyers and an aircraft carrier (with two more under construction). China has built a capable air force focusing on modern fighter aircraft with advanced air-to-air missiles, glass cockpits, long-range surface-to-air missiles (SAMs), and precision air-to-ground munitions. Although China's efforts to develop long-range power projection capabilities lagged behind its A2/AD developments, it recently purchased Russian-made heavy lift transport aircraft and developed a domestically produced model. China has purchased three aerial-refueling tankers from Ukraine to augment its limited domestically made tanker fleet of ten aircraft.[6]

Taken together, these developments pose a growing challenge to U.S. force projection capabilities in the Western Pacific.

Russia Has Streamlined Its Military Forces and Made Them More Capable

The Russian Federation inherited a military establishment of considerable size when the Soviet Union dissolved in 1992, but the political, social, and fiscal realities of the post–Cold War environment soon forced Russian leaders to attempt institutional reforms. The Russian government made several attempts over the next decade and a half to reduce the size of its military establishment and modernize its forces, but all of these efforts failed, largely because of political strife and financial constraints. The Russian armed forces remained bloated, antiquated, poorly trained, and poorly equipped.

This changed dramatically after the 2008 war with Georgia. Although Russian leaders trumpeted their victory in the conflict, the poor performance of their military forces provided an impetus for undertaking aggressive military reforms. With unusual candor, government and military officials from then-President Dmitry Medvedev on down conceded that Russia's armed forces "were in need of a mas-

---

[6] Heginbotham et al., 2015, pp. 29–34.

sive overhaul."[7] As a result, President Medvedev and Defense Minister Anatoliy Serdyukov developed a plan to create permanent combat-ready military units, improve command and control, bolster personnel training, equip the armed forces with new weapons, and increase salaries and benefits for military members—marking the most-radical reforms to the Russian military since 1945.[8] Serdyukov stressed that the reforms were intended to transform Russia's military from a mass mobilization army to "a performance-capable, mobile, and maximally armed army and navy ready to participate in three regional and local conflicts, at a minimum."[9]

In early 2009, a series of sweeping reforms began. Russian leaders redistricted the national command structure, narrowing the military span of control, and reorganized the command and control of its military forces to facilitate joint operations.[10] The reforms eliminated numbered armies, divisions, and regiments, creating a new three-tier command structure around military districts, operational commands, and brigades.[11] As this reorganization took place, many skeletal units were disestablished, installations closed, and personnel and equipment consolidated to form fully manned and equipped units. Where Russia had 203 divisions on paper in 2008, it had only 85 brigades when the reorganization was completed in December 2009. According to the Ministry of Defense, these 85 brigades were manned and equipped to be in a state of "permanent readiness."[12]

---

[7] Matthew Kosnik, "Russia's Military Reform: Putin's Last Card," *Journal of Military and Strategic Studies*, Vol. 17, No. 1, 2016.

[8] Roger McDermott, "Russia's Conventional Armed Forces and the Georgian War," *Parameters*, Vol. 39, No. 1, Spring 2009; Jim Nichol, *Russian Military Reform and Defense Policy*, Washington, D.C.: Congressional Research Service, R42006, August 24, 2011, p. 5; Athena Bryce-Rogers, "Russian Military Reform in the Aftermath of the 2008 Russia-Georgian War," *Demokratizatsiya: The Journal of Post-Soviet Democratization*, Vol. 2, No. 3, 2013.

[9] Nichol, 2011, p. 5.

[10] Nichol, 2011, pp. 5, 11.

[11] Dale Herspring, "Russian Military Reform and Anatoly Serdyukov," *Problems of Post-Communism*, Vol. 55, No. 6, November/December 2008; McDermott, 2009; Nichol, 2011, p. 6; Bryce-Rogers, 2013.

[12] Nichol, 2011, pp. 6, 14; Bryce-Rogers, 2013.

Another objective of the reforms was to improve the quality of Russia's military personnel. Russia entered the Georgia war with a top-heavy force of far too many officers and not enough properly trained enlisted personnel. After the war, Serdyukov reduced the armed forces from 1.2 million in 2008 to fewer than 1 million in 2012, with the bulk of the cuts coming from the officer corps, which was reduced from 350,000 to 150,000. Meanwhile, the reformers set out to develop a corps of skilled noncommissioned officers (NCOs) to take up leadership positions in technical specialties, such as motor rifle, reconnaissance, and transportation.[13] In mid-2017, Russia was just short of meeting its goal of having 384,000 NCOs and lower enlisted personnel under contract.[14]

The third major objective of the reform effort was to modernize and rearm Russia's military forces for 21st-century warfare. In 2006, President Vladimir Putin stated that Russia would spend the equivalent of $189 billion from 2007 to 2015 to modernize the armed forces, 45 percent of which would go into weapon systems. After the poor performance in Georgia, Russian military spending accelerated substantially, rising 27 percent in 2009 alone.[15] In December 2010, then–Prime Minister Putin announced a $698 billion procurement plan designed to upgrade or replace 11 percent of Russia's military equipment each year, with a final goal of increasing the proportion of modern weaponry to 70 percent by 2020.[16] This plan focused on upgrading nuclear weapons and delivery systems, building fifth-generation fighter aircraft and new ships and submarines, and improving digital communications and intelligence capabilities.

Russian leaders have made spotty progress in obtaining these goals. Flush with cash from soaring oil and gas prices from 2009 to 2014, Moscow committed an increasing amount of Russia's rising gross domestic product to military spending, going from an estimated

---

[13] Nichol, 2011, p. 17.

[14] IISS, "Russia and Eurasia," *The Military Balance*, Vol. 118, 2018, p. 172.

[15] Bryce-Rogers, 2013.

[16] Nichol, 2011, p. 21.

3.54 percent in 2010 to a peak of 4.84 percent in 2015 before declining to 4.17 percent 2017.[17] All of the military services benefited from this increased spending, replacing dated and often unserviceable equipment with new or at least updated items while reducing force structure overall.

With the collapse of oil and gas prices in 2014 and the economic sanctions imposed for its behavior in Ukraine, it remains to be seen whether Russia can sustain its military spending in the years ahead. Nevertheless, Russia's military performance in Syria and Ukraine suggest that its forces are much more capable than they were during the Georgia war. Russian forces have demonstrated a notable ability to conduct joint expeditionary operations integrating fixed- and rotary-wing operations and missile strikes with ground forces, although the range and complexity of the operations they have undertaken do not yet compare with those that U.S. forces can conduct.

Future Projection: Chinese Capabilities Will Almost Certainly Improve in the Next Ten to 15 Years, but Russia's Future Progress Is Less Assured

China's military capabilities are clearly on an upward trajectory. The PLA has a well-articulated military doctrine, and the Chinese government provides the military with ample economic resources despite facing increasing levels of debt. China should be expected to continue adding precision-guided missiles, advanced combat aircraft, and modern submarines and surface combatants to its arsenal, and it will soon be adding more-exotic weapons as well. In June 2017, China announced that it had developed a hypersonic ramjet that could be mated with a wide range of weapon systems.[18] Later that December, China also successfully conducted flight tests of the DF-17 ballistic

---

[17] Russia's defense spending in 2018 is projected to be at 3.90 percent of gross domestic product. See IISS, "Russia and Eurasia," Vol. 117, 2017, p. 191; IISS, 2018, p. 175.

[18] Gianpaulo Colitti, "China Unveils Its New Hypervelocity Missile Programme," *UK Defence Journal*, June 13, 2017.

missile, a weapon system designed to deliver hypersonic glide vehicles.[19] Hypersonic weapons present whole new challenges to U.S. forces operating in the Western Pacific. With velocities that exceed five times the speed of sound and with capabilities for maneuvering, these weapons will be able to penetrate existing missile defenses and dramatically reduce the time available for defending forces to detect and respond to attacks.[20] In addition to being better armed, PLA forces are also getting more competent. As a result of the experience they are gaining in distant naval deployments, airpower projection in the South China Sea, and increasingly realistic exercises, China's military personnel are becoming ever more confident.[21] Should China attempt to project force against the United States or its friends and allies, it will face some of the A2/AD challenges that its potential adversaries face.[22] However, the overarching trend suggests that Chinese forces will be increasingly able to carry out effective A2/AD and force projection missions in future scenarios.

Russia is also developing hypersonic missiles,[23] but the future of Russian military capability is not as clear. Moscow has made notable progress in its efforts to reform its military establishment, but significant challenges remain—most prominently fiscal ones. The result of the 2014 collapse of oil and gas prices in conjunction with economic sanctions has been a depressed Russian economy coupled with high inflation. Russian leaders continued their support for military reform despite these setbacks with strong defense budgets in 2015 and 2016,

---

[19] Jamie Seidel, "Hypervelocity Missile Breakthrough Makes China the World Leader in New Weaponry," news.com.au, December 31, 2017.

[20] Richard H. Speier, George Narcouzi, Carrie Lee, and Richard M. Moore, *Hypersonic Missile Nonproliferation: Hindering the Spread of a New Class of Weapons*, Santa Monica, Calif.: RAND Corporation, RR-2137-CC, 2017.

[21] Heginbotham et al., 2015, pp. 34–35.

[22] For more on the A2/AD challenges facing China, see Terrence K. Kelly, David C. Gompert, and Duncan Long, *Smarter Power, Stronger Partners*, Volume I: *Exploiting U.S. Advantages to Prevent Aggression*, Santa Monica, Calif.: RAND Corporation, RR-1359-A, 2016.

[23] Kelsey D. Atherton, "Don't Believe the Hype About Russia's Hypersonic Missile," *Popular Science*, June 18, 2017; "Russia 'Test-Fires Hypersonic Kinzal Missile,'" BBC News, March 11, 2018.

but spending declined somewhat in 2017, and Western analysts question how long Moscow can continue aggressive modernization in the current economic climate while prosecuting military operations in Syria and Ukraine.[24]

Efforts to reform Russia's military also face significant cultural and demographic challenges. The reorganization has not been completely successful; efforts to structure the force around modular brigades faced resistance from military leaders acculturated in an organizational tradition featuring heavy divisions. Consequently, some brigades had been reconsolidated into divisions or reorganized as regiments by 2017.[25] Russia also has struggled to attract enough qualified candidates to meet contract enlistment goals. [26] Russia's pool of qualified military-aged labor has shrunk over the past decade as a downstream result of a national decline in population from 1991 to 2009. Poor public images of military life and low levels of "civic loyalty" in some parts of the country have made recruitment quotas even harder to fill and have also contributed to a rise in draft dodging.[27]

Finally, efforts to modernize Russia's military equipment face constraints on several fronts. Few graduates from schools at home or abroad find the Russian defense industry an attractive source of employment. As a result, more than 50 percent of researchers in that field are now over the age of 50.[28] Arms manufacturers fill some technology gaps by importing advanced systems from abroad or obtaining licensing rights to manufacture them in Russia, but Western sanctions and export controls on critical technologies have hindered these efforts. There also has been little recapitalization in the military industrial sector since the fall of the Soviet Union. Approximately 75 percent of all manufactur-

---

[24] For example, see Kosnik, 2016; and Susanna Oxenstierna, "Russian Defence Spending and the Economic Decline," *Journal of Eurasian Studies*, Vol. 7, No. 1, January 2016.

[25] Keir Giles, *Assessing Russia's Reorganized and Rearmed Military*, Washington, D.C.: Carnegie Endowment for World Peace, task force white paper, May 3, 2017.

[26] IISS, 2018, p. 172.

[27] Kosnik, 2016.

[28] Roger Roffey, "Russian Science and Technology Is Still Having Problems—Implications for Defense Research," *Journal of Slavic Military Studies*, Vol. 26, No. 2, 2013.

ing facilities are obsolete, and 50 percent are worn out.[29] As a result, although Russia has made notable progress in its efforts to modernize its military equipment, the few new aircraft produced—e.g., Su-34s and Su-35s—have been almost entirely based on Soviet-era designs.[30]

Implications for the U.S. Air Force and the Future of Warfare

The United States has long relied on the qualitative edge that its military forces possess to offset local numerical advantages enjoyed by regional adversaries. That edge is progressively narrowing—particularly in the Western Pacific, where Chinese forces have developed a doctrine to defeat U.S. force projection efforts and the advanced systems needed to put it into action. The risks that this shift in the balance of power presents are obvious: It will be more difficult to deter China from acting aggressively in disputed territories around its periphery and more difficult to defeat Chinese forces if deterrence fails. This is particularly threatening to the USAF, with assets concentrated on several large bases on the Japanese islands of Honshu and Okinawa within range of hundreds of precision-guided MRBMs and even greater numbers of air- and ground-launched cruise missiles. USAF and naval air power would also be challenged by increasingly capable SAMs and air-defense fighters in the event of war with China. The addition of hypersonic weapons will further complicate these challenges.

The implications for the United States and the North Atlantic Treaty Organization (NATO) in Europe are less clear. Russia has improved its forces significantly since 2008, but its force numbers are still only a fraction of those of NATO when viewed as a whole and possess less capability.[31] As mentioned in the previous section,

---

[29] Roffey, 2013.

[30] Roffey, 2013.

[31] See Scott Boston, Michael Johnson, Nathan Beauchamp-Mustafaga, and Yvonne K. Crane, *Assessing the Conventional Force Imbalance in Europe: Implications for Countering Russian Local Superiority*, Santa Monica, Calif.: RAND Corporation, RR-2402, 2018.

Russia faces a series of economic, demographic, and technological challenges. Although its population and economy are no longer declining, growth remains stagnant, and the aging problems and lack of recapitalization and innovation will likely constrain its military development.

Russia, nonetheless, will continue to possess several military advantages over NATO, particularly when operating close to its borders in its "near abroad." Many European countries shed their heavy mechanized forces to better conduct expeditionary counterterrorism operations, but Russia has retained the ability to conduct combined arms maneuver warfare.[32] Russia's integrated air defense system will prevent fourth-generation NATO aircraft from flying over Eastern Europe during the early days of a conflict.[33] Above all, Russia possesses geographic advantages and could mobilize sufficient forces to strike at areas near its borders (e.g., the Baltics) before the United States and NATO could deploy the forces needed to effectively defend them.[34] It has not done so already, presumably, because Russian leaders are intimidated by U.S. conventional precision-strike capabilities, because they realize that Russia would likely lose the longer war if the United States and NATO were to hold together and fight back, or simply because they do not view such a conventional attack as being in its national interest at the present time.[35] If Russian military reforms continue, or Russia's political calculus changes, that dynamic could change.

The modernization and professionalization of the Chinese and Russian forces should drive further USAF investments in several

---

[32] Michael Shurkin, *The Abilities of the British, French, and German Armies to Generate and Sustain Armored Brigades in the Baltics*, Santa Monica, Calif.: RAND Corporation, RR-1629-A, 2017; Boston et al., 2018, p. 5.

[33] Boston et al., 2018, pp. 8–18.

[34] Shlapak and Johnson, 2016.

[35] Richard Sokolsky, *The New NATO-Russia Military Balance: Implications for European Security*, Washington, D.C.: Carnegie Endowment for World Peace, task force white paper, March 13, 2017.

areas.[36] First, the USAF will need to address the growing threat posed by both Chinese and Russian air defense systems. Second, particularly because of the Chinese MRBM threat to USAF bases in the Western Pacific, the USAF will need to increase its operational resilience by investing in air defenses, by dispersing its forces to operate out of multiple smaller bases when possible, and by operating at longer ranges outside the effective radius of these missiles. Third, the USAF will need to boost its investments in both training and munitions for striking conventional targets—regardless of whether these are land-based armor formations for a European scenario or maritime targets for a Western Pacific scenario. Finally, the USAF needs to focus on increased awareness of both Chinese and Russian military movements. As the balance of forces shifts in Chinese and Russian favor, either power (or both) might be more willing to risk an overt military confrontation.

In the meantime, China and Russia are more likely to pursue their objectives along the lines of a trend discussed in Chapter Five: operating in the gray zone and relying on incremental aggression or using covert military forces.

---

[36] For a detailed analysis of possible investments, see Chapters Two and Three of Ochmanek et al., 2017; and David Ochmanek, *Restoring U.S. Power Projection Capabilities: Responding to the 2018 National Defense Strategy*, Santa Monica, Calif.: RAND Corporation, PE-260-AF, 2018.

CHAPTER FOUR

Trend 3: The Development of Asymmetric Strategies by Second-Tier Powers

Context: Iran's and North Korea's Conventional Military Capabilities Are Stagnating

While the military forces of near-peer competitors are becoming more capable, Iran's and North Korea's conventional military capabilities are, in many respects, stagnating. To compensate for these problems, both countries have developed asymmetric strategies and niche capabilities in efforts to offset superior U.S. and allied forces. This will likely be a growing trend in the next ten to 15 years.

Historical Trend: Both Nations Have Large Forces, but They Are Outdated and Substandard

The Islamic Republic of Iran maintains a formidable conventional military force on paper. With more than 1,500 main battle tanks, more than 6,798 artillery pieces, 334 combat capable aircraft, more than 300 naval surface combatants, 21 submarines, and more than a half-million active-duty personnel, Iran's military capabilities are among the most formidable in the Middle East.[1] However, these numbers do not tell the whole story. Of Iran's 523,000 active-duty soldiers, only about 125,000 of them belong to the better-trained and better-equipped Islamic Revolutionary Guard Corps (IRGC).[2] Moreover, after many

---

[1] IISS, "Middle East and North Africa," *The Military Balance*, Vol. 118, 2018, pp. 333–337.

[2] IISS, 2018, p. 337.

years of economic sanctions and weapon embargoes, Iranian military forces are operating increasingly outdated equipment. Of the Iranian army's large inventory of main battle tanks, its most modern are a few hundred 1970s-era T-72s; the rest are even earlier platforms.[3] Similarly, the Iranian air force consists of a mixture of third- and fourth-generation Soviet, U.S., and French aircraft, but only 60–80 percent of them are believed to be serviceable as a result of the sanctions.[4] Finally, of Iran's many naval surface combatant vessels, almost all of them are coastal patrol craft and fast attack boats—the Iranian navy's largest surface combatants consists of five frigates.

Similarly, the Democratic People's Republic of Korea has sizable conventional military forces, but its military capabilities are also eroding under the weight of extended economic sanctions. Despite an estimated 1.28 million active-duty military personnel, North Korea's conventional military is an increasingly hollow force with underfed soldiers and obsolete equipment.[5] Its most modern tank, the Soviet-era T-62, was first produced in the early 1960s. Although North Korea has a regiment of fourth-generation MiG-29 fighters, its most common aircraft are 1950s-era IL-28s, MiG-17s and MiG-21s.[6] Despite severe fuel shortages in the civilian economy, North Korea has stockpiled a considerable volume of fuel and more than a million tons of ammunition in war reserve, but it is questionable whether it has the logistical capacity to adequately supply its forces in extended combat.[7] Finally, although the North Korean army is the fourth largest in the world, its soldiers are believed to suffer from malnutrition even in peacetime as a result of the country's recurring food shortages.[8]

---

[3] IISS, 2018, p. 334.

[4] IISS, 2018, p. 336.

[5] IISS, "Asia," *The Military Balance*, Vol. 117, 2017, p. 303.

[6] IISS, "Asia," *The Military Balance*, Vol. 118, 2018, p. 277.

[7] Andrew Scobell and John M. Sanford, *North Korea's Military Threat: Pyongyang's Conventional Forces, Weapons of Mass Destruction, and Ballistic Missiles*, Carlisle, Pa.: Strategic Studies Institute, April 2007, pp. 62–63.

[8] Scobell and Sanford, 2007, pp. 63, 69; Eleanor Ross, "North Korea Military: What to Know About Life as a Soldier in Kim Jong Un's Army," *Newsweek*, June 21, 2017.

Future Projection: Iran and North Korea Will Increasingly Rely on Asymmetric Strategies to Offset Their Conventional Vulnerabilities

To compensate for their conventional vulnerabilities, both powers have developed asymmetric strategies and niche capabilities that they are likely to rely on increasingly over the next ten to 15 years. Iran exploits its geographical proximity to the Persian Gulf and Strait of Hormuz to hold U.S. interests at risk and to threaten the security of other actors transiting those waters. Iran has developed a strategy of using its craft to sow mines in critical waterways, attack ships transiting there, and even conduct swarm attacks on U.S. Navy warships if necessary. Iran also has expanded its area-denial capabilities. For instance, it acquired a Russian S-300 anti-aircraft system to deny access to the airspace in selected areas (such as the capital, its nuclear development sites, and the Strait of Hormuz) and has invested in a variety of other weapons, from advanced mines to anti-ship missiles, to target vessels transiting the Strait.[9] Finally, Iran has a growing arsenal of UAVs (for remotely striking operational targets in the region) and SRBMs, MRBMs, and IRBMs (able to strike as far as Eastern Europe).[10]

North Korea also exploits a geographical advantage—in its case, the fact that Seoul is only about 35 miles from the demilitarized zone (DMZ), within striking range of North Korean rockets and boosted artillery shells. Capitalizing on this vulnerability, North Korea has

---

[9] Dave Majumdar, "Could Iran Sink a U.S. Navy Aircraft Carrier?" *National Interest*, December 30, 2015; Associated Press, "Iran Deploys Air Defense System Around Fordo Nuclear Site," *New York Times*, August 29, 2016; Franz-Stefan Gady, "Iran: Russian-Made S-300 Air Defense Missile Systems Placed on 'Combat Duty,'" *The Diplomat*, July 11, 2017; Elad Benari, "Pentagon: Iran Has Deployed the S-300 System," *Arutz Sheva*, March 8, 2018.

[10] Hilary Clarke and Shirzad Bozorgmehr, "Iran Unveils New Long-Range Ballistic Missile," CNN, September 23, 2017; IISS, 2018, p. 335. Given the conventional warfighting skills that elements of the IRGC and Quds Force developed in Syria and the power vacuum created by U.S. withdrawals from the region, it is worth noting that Tehran might decide to develop more-substantial conventional capabilities. Recent Iranian interest in purchasing advanced Russian combat aircraft suggests that Iranian leaders might be considering this option. See Franz-Stefan Gady, "Iran, Russia Inching Closer to Su-30 Fighter Jet Deal," *The Diplomat*, December 1, 2016.

invested the hills near the DMZ with large numbers of long-range artillery, rockets, and missiles dug into caves and revetments to make them difficult to find and destroy. By some estimates, North Korea could bombard Seoul with more than half a million shells just on the first day of a conflict.[11] The regime has a special operations force of approximately 88,000 soldiers trained to conduct reconnaissance and sabotage missions behind South Korean lines.[12] Like Iran, North Korea invested in conventional SRBMs, MRBMs, and IRBMs that could attack U.S. bases in the region or cities in South Korea and Japan. The North Korean navy's principal surface combatants consist of only two frigates, but it has 73 submarines and nearly 400 coastal patrol vessels and fast attack boats.[13] By some estimates, North Korea produces thousands of tons of chemical weapons, including such deadly nerve agents as sarin and VX. Analysts worry that if war with South Korea were to occur, the bombardment of Seoul would feature not only conventional shells and warheads but also chemical ones.[14]

Implications for the U.S. Air Force and the Future of Warfare

The need to counter Iran's and North Korea's asymmetric strategies will put specialized demands on U.S. forces. Given the high lethality of some of these capabilities (particularly North Korea's chemical and nuclear weapons—and possibly Iran's, if it develops comparable weapons in the next ten to 15 years), the United States will need to focus on developing tools to neutralize them. U.S. forces will need to employ these capabilities early on in a conflict, before the regime can

---

[11] Dave Majumdar, "5 North Korean Weapons South Korea Should Fear," *The National Interest*, January 6, 2016; Kyle Mizokami, "Could North Korea Annihilate Seoul with Its Artillery?" *The National Interest*, April 25, 2017.

[12] Barbara Starr, "Pentagon: North Korean Special Forces 'Highly Trained, Well-Equipped,'" CNN, February 12, 2016.

[13] IISS, 2018, p. 276.

[14] Majumdar, 2016.

strike the United States or one of its regional allies and partners. Iran's and North Korea's asymmetric investments pose other challenges, too. The United States will need more-advanced antimine and antisubmarine warfare capabilities, and the Navy will need ship-defense weapons that can quickly acquire, target, and destroy small, fast-moving vessels, shifting from one target to the next at high rates of speed. The USAF will need more-advanced electronic warfare, longer-range standoff weapons to defeat advanced IADS, more capability to strike deeply buried facilities, and more capable ISR—including, potentially, more special operations forces—to locate chemical and nuclear storage facilities, hidden artillery, and mobile missile launchers. And of course, all U.S. forces will need more-effective missile defenses.

CHAPTER FIVE

Trend 4: Potential Adversaries' Increasing Use of "Gray Zone" Tactics

Context: U.S. Adversaries That Could Not Directly Challenge U.S. Conventional Military Power Developed Gray-Zone Strategies

Since the beginning of the post–Cold War era, U.S. adversaries could not directly challenge U.S. conventional military power. Instead, they developed gray-zone strategies, employing such tactics as proxy groups and covert military forces to obtain objectives while staying below the threshold of U.S. military response. The need to counter gray-zone strategies will be a significant challenge for the United States in the next ten to 15 years.

Historical Trend: Each U.S. Adversary Tailored Gray-Zone Strategies to Its Particular Objectives

China, Russia, Iran, and North Korea have all developed different flavors of gray-zone strategies based on their own interests and abilities, but they share one common factor: They are all pursuing interests that threaten the United States or its regional allies.[1]

China relies heavily on a gray-zone strategy using what is often described as *salami tactics*—taking a little at a time to avoid triggering

---

[1] The authors owe an intellectual debt to Brad Roberts, whose 2016 book identified these gray-zone strategies, which it described as "theories of victory." See Brad Roberts, *The Case for U.S. Nuclear Weapons in the 21st Century*, Stanford, Calif.: Stanford University Press, 2016.

strong military resistance—to assert its territorial claims in the South China Sea.[2] Beijing's artificial island-building in the disputed waters of the South China Sea and its rapid militarization of those outposts are examples of the use of the gray-zone tactic of creeping expansionism in which China's actions are incrementally changing the territorial status quo.[3] China has also used its commercial fishing fleets as proxies to drive out the fishing fleets of other states in disputed waters. When opposing fishermen try to fight back, China's coast guard, Marine Surveillance Agency, and Fisheries Law Enforcement Agency appear on the scene to intimidate or even arrest them. These law enforcement "white hulls" are often backed up at a distance by gray-hulled PLA Navy vessels.[4]

Russia also uses gray-zone strategies to ensure that the states on its borders (1) do not embrace policies that Russia considers hostile or (2) become too closely aligned with the West. It uses nonmilitary tools of coercion—such as cyberattacks, propaganda, economic levers, and covert operations—to conduct political warfare while circumventing U.S. and NATO responses.[5] For instance, when Estonia moved a memorial commemorating Soviet sacrifice in World War II from the center of Tallinn in April 2007, it experienced one of the most intense denial-of-service attacks in history, lasting almost three weeks and

---

[2]   For the seminal work on the use of salami tactics, see Thomas C. Schelling, *Arms and Influence*, New Haven, Conn.: Yale University Press, 1966, p. 68.

[3]   As will be discussed in this chapter, Chinese leaders first said that no military capabilities would be put on the artificial islands, but the PLA has progressively developed them into substantial air and naval bases. Although these installations contribute to China's growing force deployment capabilities, they would be vulnerable to U.S. and allied A2/AD capabilities. See Kelly et al., 2016, p. 106; Jesse Johnson, "China Confirms Deployment of Fighters to South China Sea Island for the First Time," *Japan Times*, December 2, 2017; Bethlehem Feleke, "China Tests Bombers on South China Sea Island," CNN, May 21, 2018.

[4]   For a discussion, see Ryan D. Martinson, "The Arming of China's Maritime Frontier," *China Maritime Report*, No. 2, June 2017.

[5]   Linda Robinson, Todd C. Helmus, Raphael S. Cohen, Alireza Nader, Andrew Radin, Madeline Magnuson, and Katya Migacheva, *Modern Political Warfare: Current Practices and Possible Responses*, Santa Monica, Calif.: RAND Corporation, RR-1772-A, 2017. Also see Raphael S. Cohen and Andrew Radin, *Russian Hostile Measures*, Santa Monica, Calif.: RAND Corporation, RR-1793-A, 2019.

taking 58 Estonian websites, including that of its largest bank, offline for various periods of time.[6] The attack was carried out by civilian hacker groups in Russia, but the Estonian government claimed those groups were directed by the Kremlin.[7]

Russia also relies on covert military action to carry out its gray-zone strategy, particularly in Ukraine. The expression "little green men" refers to Russia's green uniform–clad special forces who occupied Crimea in a rapid, mostly bloodless operation in 2014.[8] By not wearing any identification, they provided Russia with plausible deniability; by avoiding large-scale bloodshed, they undercut NATO's willingness to respond with force.[9] By the time Ukraine and NATO were willing to act, Russia's annexation of Crimea was complete. Russia attempted this tactic again in the Donbas region of eastern Ukraine, where Russian special operators organized and armed local separatist movements, forming pro-Russian militias, only to find themselves—along with an estimated 40,000 Russian "volunteers" and 5,000 soldiers—bogged down in a bloody conflict against the Ukrainian military.[10]

Iran also relies on covert military action and proxies to protect itself from regime change and external threats, reduce U.S. influence in the Middle East, empower other Shiite regimes and factions, and undermine its principal regional rivals, Saudi Arabia and Israel. Iran supports and directs proxy terrorist and insurgent groups, such as Lebanese Hezbollah, Kata'ib Hizballah in Iraq, Hamas, Palestinian Islamic Jihad, and others.[11] Iran has used the Syrian conflict as a laboratory for

---

[6] Thomas Rid, "Cyber War Will Not Take Place," *Journal of Strategic Studies*, Vol. 35, No. 1, February 2012.

[7] Rid, 2012, pp. 11–12.

[8] Heidi Reisinger and Aleksandr Golts, *Russia's Hybrid Warfare: Waging War Below the Radar of Traditional Collective Defence*, Rome: NATO Defense College, Research Paper No. 105, November 2014.

[9] Reisinger and Golts, 2014, pp. 5–6.

[10] Christopher Miller, "Anxious Ukraine Risks Escalation in 'Creeping Offensive,'" Radio Free Europe/Radio Liberty, January 30, 2017.

[11] Bureau of Counterterrorism and Countering Violent Extremism, *Country Reports on Terrorism 2015*, Washington, D.C.: U.S. Department of State, June 2016.

developing new ways to project power through its proxy forces. Since October 2015, Iran has sent cadres of IRGC officers and NCOs to organize and lead Syrian, Iraqi, and Hezbollah militia units in combat in ways previously not seen. As Paul Bucala and Frederick W. Kagan point out, "If the IRGC has, indeed, mastered this ability, then it has positioned itself to use small numbers of conventional forces on foreign battlefields to produce effects disproportionate to their size."[12]

North Korea's interests—preserving the Pyongyang regime and reuniting the Korean peninsula under its authority—outstrip its stagnating conventional capabilities. North Korea cannot defeat South Korean and U.S. forces in conventional warfare, so it has employed a strategy of persistent, low-level provocations to test and erode the South's resistance. One of the deadliest of these provocations was North Korea's torpedoing of the South Korean destroyer *Cheonan* on March 26, 2010.[13] North Korea has also bombarded disputed islands in South Korea at semiregular intervals, often eliciting a South Korean bombardment but no decisive action in response.[14] In addition, North Korea has conducted nonkinetic attacks; in 2013, Pyongyang conducted a denial-of-service attack on three South Korean television stations and a bank.[15] In 2016, North Korea is believed to have hacked more than 140,000 computers across 160 South Korean companies and government agencies, presumably as part of a concerted campaign of industrial and military espionage.[16] In December 2016, news

---

[12] Paul Bucala and Frederick W. Kagan, *Iran's Evolving Way of War: How the IRGC Fights in Syria*, Washington, D.C.: Critical Threats Project, March 15, 2016, p. 2.

[13] "North Korea: 'No Apology' for S Korea Cheonan Sinking," BBC News, March 24, 2015.

[14] See James Pearson and Ju-Min Park, "The War That Never Ends Between the Koreas," Reuters, June 16, 2014.

[15] Julian Ryall, "North Korea Waging 'Cyber Warfare' Against South by Spreading Malicious Rumours," *Telegraph*, October 25, 2016.

[16] Jack Kim, "North Korea Mounts Long-Running Hack of South Korea Computers, Says Seoul," Reuters, June 13, 2016.

accounts reported that North Korea might have even breached South Korea's cyber command.[17]

North Korea's provocations present a different challenge than the gray-zone actions carried out by the other three actors. Unlike China's building of islands in the South China Sea, Russia's use of "little green men" in Ukraine, or even Iran's use of proxy forces, North Korea's actions are often blatantly aggressive and openly defiant of international agreements. As a result, U.S. and South Korean leaders have struggled to find punitive responses that are just severe enough to deter further North Korean provocation without creating or escalating a crisis.

Future Projection: Opponents Will Likely Continue Using Gray-Zone Strategies in the Next Ten to 15 Years

All four of these states will likely continue using gray-zone strategies in the coming years, but they will do so for different reasons. Iranian and North Korean conventional capabilities are deteriorating, so gray-zone strategies are the most promising alternatives. Tehran, in particular, has found these strategies to be very successful. Thanks to U.S. intervention and Iranian behind-the-scenes influence, Iran's most threatening neighbor, the Baathist Sunni government of Iraq, was replaced with an Iran-friendly Shiite government, and the most recent parliamentary election in Iraq has brought to power the political party of longtime U.S. adversary Shia militia leader Moqtada al-Sadr.[18] Meanwhile, in Syria, Iranian proxies have helped defeat the "Islamic State" and defended the Bashar al-Assad regime from other rebel groups. As

---

[17] "North Korea Hacks South's Military Cyber Command," BBC News, December 6, 2016; "N. Korea Likely Hacked S. Korea Cyber Command: Military," Yonhap News, December 6, 2016.

[18] Tim Arango, "Iran Dominates in Iraq After the U.S. 'Handed the Country Over,'" *New York Times*, July 15, 2017; Manish Rai, "Iraq Is a Client State of Iran," *International Policy Digest*, November 9, 2017; Isaac Kfir, "Iraq as a 'Client State' of Iran," *The Strategist*, March 7, 2018; Raya Jalabi and Michael Gregory, "Cleric Moqtada al-Sadr's Block Wins Iraqi Election," Reuters, May 18, 2018.

IRGC forces further develop their cadre operations abroad, they could use them in "expeditionary operations in other theaters, such as Iraq, Yemen, and Lebanon, where there are already large groups of allies and proxy militias."[19]

North Korea's tactic of persistent provocation, on the other hand, has not been particularly successful in achieving Pyongyang's objective of wearing down South Korea's will to resist. Although some citizens in the South were encouraged by the relative thaw in relations around the 2018 Winter Olympics, opinion polls taken shortly thereafter indicate there was still considerable distrust of Pyongyang.[20] Those polls shifted somewhat after President Moon Jae-in met with Kim Jong-un in the DMZ in April 2018 and during the run-up to the first summit with President Trump, but the shift can be attributed more to South Koreans' hopes for peace than to a loss of national resolve to resist northern aggression.[21] Importantly, North Korea has not conducted any violent provocations since the meetings with Moon and Trump began. It remains to be seen whether such restraint will continue if the negotiations fall through or if they do not result in the economic, diplomatic, and military concessions that Pyongyang is likely to demand. Given its violent history and the fact that North Korea lacks the conventional capabilities to obtain its objectives by direct force, it is likely to resume its long-term gray-zone strategy.

China and Russia will also probably continue their gray-zone strategies, although both states' conventional capabilities will likely grow during the next ten to 15 years—especially China's. Neither nation relishes a direct military confrontation with the United States, making gray-zone operations more attractive for anything short of an extreme contingency. China's tactic of incremental aggression in the South China Sea has been quite successful. China first began dredging sand onto reefs

[19] Bucala and Kagan, 2016, p. 2.

[20] Choe San-Hun, "Reunification with North Korea Unappealing for Younger South Koreans," *The Star*, January 28, 2018; Clint Work, "What Do Younger South Koreans Think of North Korea?" *The Diplomat*, February 2, 2018.

[21] "Majority of South Koreans Feel That North Korean Attitude Is Changing," *Hankoreh*, March 18, 2018.

to build the artificial islands in support of its territorial claims there in 2014. In 2015, President Xi Jinping assured then-President Barack Obama that China had no intent to militarize the islands. But by 2017, China was building infrastructure on these islands capable of supporting military aircraft. Since then, the PLA Air Force has landed fighters on some of the islands and installed radar-jamming equipment and missiles there.[22] In May 2018, China announced that it had landed H-6K bombers on Woody Island in the Spratlys.[23] Given China's success in the South China Sea, there is no reason to expect Beijing to change its strategy in the next ten to 15 years unless militarily confronted by the United States.

Russia has been less successful in Eastern Ukraine but will also probably continue using gray-zone strategies. When conflicts involving Soviet-supported (and, later, Russian-supported) separatist movements in the Nagorno-Karabakh region of Azerbaijan and the Abkhazia and South Ossetia regions of Georgia bogged down in the late 1980s and early 1990s, Moscow mediated cease-fires between the belligerents, creating "frozen conflicts" in which active fighting was suspended without peace agreements. When Georgia took steps toward joining NATO in 2008, Russia resumed its agitation in Abkhazia and South Ossetia and ultimately intervened with conventional military forces on the separatists' behalf when Georgia attempted to rein in the wayward regions. It is debatable whether Eastern Ukraine is now a frozen conflict—repeated cease-fire agreements have failed and low-level fighting continues—but separatist forces effectively control the Donbas region and analysts observe that Russia can conserve its resources and wait for better conditions to escalate the fight.[24]

Russia could attempt to use gray-zone tactics on other areas of Europe that might be vulnerable to Russian subversion. For example,

---

[22] Joseph Trevithick, "SAMs and Anti-Ship Missiles Are Now Guarding China's South China Sea Islands," *The Drive*, May 3, 2018.

[23] Felke, 2018.

[24] Robert Orttung and Christopher Walker, "Putin's Frozen Conflicts," *Foreign Policy*, February 13, 2015; L. Todd Wood, "With U.S. Distracted, Russia Warms to Opportunities in 'Frozen Conflicts,'" *Washington Times*, April 20, 2017; Alexandra Prentice, "Ukraine, Allies Fear Escalation After Russia Exits Ceasefire Group," Reuters, December 20, 2017.

both Estonia and Latvia have substantial concentrations of ethnic Russians living in their major cities and their eastern counties along the Russian border, with the density of Russian speakers exceeding 80 percent in Ida-Viru county in northeast Estonia.[25] Many of these residents have been denied state education and employment benefits because they cannot pass Estonian- or Latvian-language citizenship tests, making them vulnerable to Russian propaganda, which tells them they should consider themselves part of the "Russian world."[26] Estonian authorities claim to be addressing the grievances of its Russian population, but Latvia passed a law in April 2018 requiring secondary school students to be taught in Latvian rather than in Russian, provoking threats of economic sanction from Moscow.[27] In any case, gray-zone strategies are pernicious, and the threat to the Baltic states and other countries on Russia's periphery could easily escalate in the next ten to 15 years.

Implications for the U.S. Air Force and the Future of Warfare

Just as each opponent employs its own particular gray-zone approach, strategies to counter these activities will need to be tailored to the challenges presented. In the South China Sea, this will entail continuing to conduct—and possibly increasing—freedom-of-navigation missions in the waters and airspace that China illegally claims as its territory. In northeast Asia, South Korean forces—and U.S. forces, if attacked— will need to respond to each of the North's violent provocations with proportionate force, communicating to Pyongyang that these attacks will not break the allies' will to resist and will result in costly punishment. Defeating Russia's gray-zone strategy will require develop-

---

[25] Aimar Altosaar, "Ida-Viru County and Russia," *Maailma Vaade*, No. 24, March 5, 2018.

[26] Estonian Foreign Intelligence Service, *International Security and Estonia 2018*, Tallin, Estonia: Ministry of Defence, 2018, p. 50.

[27] Paul Goble, "Experts: Estonia Has Successfully Integrated Nearly 90% of Its Ethnic Russians," *Estonian World*, March 1, 2018; Alec Luhn, "Moscow Threatens Sanctions Against Latvia over Removal of Russian from Secondary Schools," *The Telegraph*, April 3, 2018.

ing countermeasures at multiple levels of confrontation. At the tactical level, special operations and law enforcement forces need to expose and combat Russia's "little green men" and other subversive elements operating in threatened regions. Information operations strategies need to challenge Russian propaganda and deliver progovernment narratives to at-risk populations. Most importantly, states with Russian minorities need to address these citizens' grievances and help them assimilate.[28] In the Middle East, the United States and its regional partners will need to address each conflict on a case-by-case basis, exposing Iran's role in its proxies' actions, supporting selected opposing forces, and potentially even punishing Iran for its behavior in selected cases. Overall, U.S. leaders will need to convince any potential aggressor of a willingness to confront gray-zone tactics and to defend U.S. allies if such confrontations escalate. Making such policies credible could put substantial burdens on the joint force.

All of these strategies will also put significant burdens on air and space support for high-quality ISR. Special operators and proxy groups might think they are invisible when they shed their uniforms, but cyber and signals intelligence can identify organizations and command relationships, and imagery can monitor the movement of vehicles and weapons across borders and waterways.[29] In sum, USAF ISR can provide the information needed to establish the facts on the ground (or water) to support U.S. and allied diplomatic positions, military actions, and information operations.

The rise in gray-zone strategies will also place new demands on the other parts of the joint force. Given the prominence of cyberattacks in gray-zone strategies, cyber defenses will be increasingly important for neutralizing these threats. Furthermore, given that many gray-zone strategies operate in the murky world between conflict and criminality, the joint force will need to develop mechanisms to better coordinate

---

[28] All of this refers, of course, to the destabilization and covert operations phase of Russia's gray-zone strategy. If the conflict escalates to conventional war, simply challenging Russian propaganda and attempting to address citizens' grievances will not be sufficient.

[29] Paul D. Shinkman, "Russia Has Deployed Thousands of Tanks, Troops to Ukraine, Top Official Says," *US News*, November 24, 2017.

its actions with law enforcement agencies, and there will be increased demand for forces that straddle both worlds. In the maritime domain, this could result in newfound importance for the U.S. Coast Guard. On land, this might increase the utility of gendarmerie-type forces. Above all, gray-zone strategies often focus on manipulating the information domain, so the joint force will need to rethink how it conducts information operations to be better able to expose; publicize; and, ultimately, counter these subversive actions.

CHAPTER SIX

Trend 5: A Weakening of the State's Monopoly on Violence

Context: As States Fail, Individuals and Groups Seek Weapons for Protection

According to Max Weber, a state is "a human community that (successfully) claims the monopoly of the legitimate use of physical force within a given territory."[1] The word in parentheses is significant. To remain a state, a government must be successful in the assertion of its monopoly on violence. As ever greater numbers and types of weapons become available to nonstate groups that are politically, culturally, or economically motivated, states in some parts of the world could become increasingly ungovernable. As states fail, additional individuals and groups seek weapons for the protection they once relied on states to provide, and the "democratization of violence" accelerates.[2] This phenomenon, along with two others—transnational terrorism and third-

---

[1]   Max Weber, "Politics as a Vocation," one of a series of lectures delivered to the Free Students Union, Munich, January 28, 1919.

[2]   Abdel-Fatau Musah, "Privatization of Security, Arms Proliferation, and the Process of State Collapse in Africa," *Development and Change*, Vol. 33, No. 5, 2002, pp. 911–933. The term *democratization of violence* refers to the growing ability of individuals and groups, other than state authorities, to use violence. The expression first appeared in 1958 and grew in currency throughout the Vietnam War before sharply declining in frequency in 1973. Fareed Zakaria revived it in 2003 when he used it to describe international terrorism. See Fareed Zakaria, *The Future of Freedom: Illiberal Democracy at Home and Abroad*, New York: W. W. Norton, 2003.

party state involvement in intrastate conflict—will likely continue, with implications for the future of war in the next ten to 15 years.

Historical Trend: Arms Proliferation to Nonstate Actors Fuels Democratization of Violence

The weakening or collapse of state authority in several regions of the world since the end of the Cold War has resulted in a proliferation of weapons to nonstate actors, fueling political and civil violence. This violence can be particularly intense when substate groups have access to heavy weaponry or are supported by outside actors, as occurred in the Balkans, Central Asia, and the Horn of Africa in the 1990s and as has occurred in Africa, the Middle East, southeastern Europe, and Central and South Asia since 2001.[3] The connections among arms proliferation, state failure, and the democratization of violence have been most evident in Africa: According to the Fund for Peace, the continent accounts for 24 of the world's 32 most fragile states.[4] Of the approximate 875 million small arms that are in circulation, stockpiled, in military arsenals, and in private possession worldwide, an estimated 100 million are in Africa, and two-thirds of those are in the hands of civilians and nonstate actors.[5]

The democratization of violence can also occur when lucrative illicit activities, such as narco-trafficking and human trafficking, develop in regions with weak governance. Large influxes of cash facili-

---

[3]   Michael T. Klare, "The Deadly Connection: Paramilitary Bands, Small Arms Diffusion, and State Failure," in Robert I. Rotberg, ed., *When States Fail: Causes and Consequences,* Princeton, N.J.: Princeton University Press, 2003; Josef Danczuk, "The Global Spread of Arms: The Link Between State Collapse, Small Arms Proliferation, and Global Conflict," *Military Review,* Vol. 96, No. 5, September–October 2016.

[4]   J. J. Messner, Nate Haken, Patricia Taft, Ignatius Onyekwere, Hannah Blyth, Charles Fiertz, Christina Murphy, Amanda Quinn, and McKenzie Horwitz, *2018 Fragile States Index,* Washington, D.C.: Fund For Peace, 2018.

[5]   Esther Chelule, "Proliferation of Small Arms and Light Weapons: Challenge to Development, Peace and Security in Africa," *IOSR Journal of Humanities and Social Science,* Vol. 19, No. 5, May 2014.

tate the purchase of arms, which criminal cartels procure to enforce discipline and secure their territories against rivals and state authorities. Economic and political motives can intermingle; for example, groups use illicit activities to fund violent operations in pursuit of political objectives, as occurred in Latin America, South Asia, and Southeast Asia.[6]

In some of these cases, the democratization of violence is a result of state failure. In others, it is a contributing cause of state failure. Whatever the causal relationship, it poses a persistent challenge to security and stability in several less-developed regions of the world.

Future Projection: Democratization of Violence Will Remain a Problem, with Transnational Terrorism and Third-Party State Involvement Likely Contributors

The democratization of violence will continue over the next ten to 15 years. If trends in state failure from the past decade persist, substate violence will not decline appreciably. On the other hand, the data suggest that it probably will not get much worse. As we have explained, the democratization of violence is closely tied to the inability of states to effectively govern their territories. As Figure 6.1 indicates, the numbers of failing and failed states have remained relatively stable over the past 13 years.

This figure displays data from the Fragile States Index (called the "Failed States Index" until 2014), which provides an annual measure of each state's level of fragility based on quantitative and qualitative assessments of a dozen indicators across cohesion, economic, political, and social dimensions. States are scored and sorted into categories ranging from "very high alert" (the uppermost at-risk category) to "very sustainable" (the most stable condition). Most states in the "very high alert" category are in open civil war or have governments that are failing in multiple dimensions. In 2018, these states were the Dem-

---

[6]   Emma Björnehed, "Narcoterrorism: The Merger of the War on Drugs and the War on Terrorism," *Global Crime*, Vol. 6, No. 3, November 2004.

Figure 6.1
Numbers of States in the Three Highest-Risk Categories in the Fragile States Index, 2006–2018

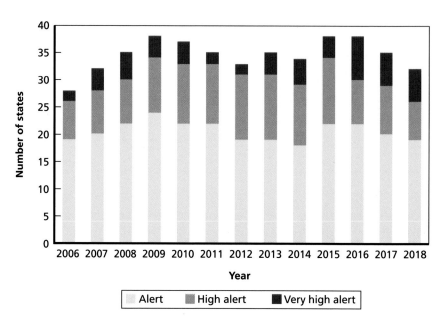

SOURCE: Fund for Peace, Fragile States Index data sets, 2006–2018.

ocratic Republic of Congo, Central African Republic, Syria, Yemen, Somalia, and South Sudan.[7] States in the "high alert" and "alert" categories have serious domestic strains but are not in as dire straits as those in the highest category. A sampling of these states would include Haiti, Iraq, and Afghanistan in the "high alert" category and Liberia, North Korea, and Pakistan in the "alert" category.

If trends from the past dozen years continue, we should expect about the same numbers of states failing or struggling to maintain order in the next ten to 15 years as we have seen in the past. This suggests that the democratization of violence in the less-developed world will continue at about the same rates. Although there is a strong correlation between state fragility and the democratization of violence,

---

[7] Messner et al., 2018.

that relationship does not explain all of the violence seen at the sub-state level; there are two other factors that might make it worse. Transnational terrorism and third-party state involvement have also played important roles in this phenomenon and will likely do so in the future.

Transnational Terrorism

As early as 1976, the Central Intelligence Agency identified transnational terrorism as a rising phenomenon, defining it as terrorism "carried out by basically autonomous nonstate actors, whether or not they enjoy some degree of support from sympathetic states."[8] Indeed, as Figure 6.2 indicates, incidents of terrorism were frequent in the late Cold War era, but declined in the 1990s before rising in 2001 and especially after 2003.

The rise and fall of the frequency of these attacks reflect changing world conditions and changing motives driving the violence. Most of the incidents from 1970 to 1992 were state-sponsored attacks related to proxy wars between the United States and Soviet Union or other Cold War–related substate conflicts. When the Cold War ended with the fall of the Soviet Union, the frequency of terrorist attacks declined, only to increase again with the rise of Islamic extremism after 2000. Although many incidents in the latter era took place in Afghanistan and Iraq, most of them did not (as the figure indicates). Still, a common thread running through all of these eras is that most terrorist attacks are related to ongoing conflicts. This is confirmed in Figure 6.3, which shows the number of terrorist attacks that have occurred in conflict countries relative to the number of attacks that have occurred in non-conflict countries in the post–Cold War era.

As the figure indicates, the numbers of terrorist attacks occurring in conflict countries and nonconflict countries were comparable from

---

[8]   Central Intelligence Agency, *International and Transnational Terrorism: Diagnosis and Prognosis*, PR 76 10030, April 1976. The same report defines *terrorism* as "the threat or use of violence for political purposes when (1) such actions are intended to influence the attitudes and behavior of a target wider than its intended victims, and (2) its ramifications transcend national boundaries (as a result, for example, the nationality or foreign ties of its perpetrators, its locale, the identity of its institutional or human victims, its declared objectives, or the mechanics of its resolution)."

Figure 6.2
Total Incidents of Terrorism, 1970–2010

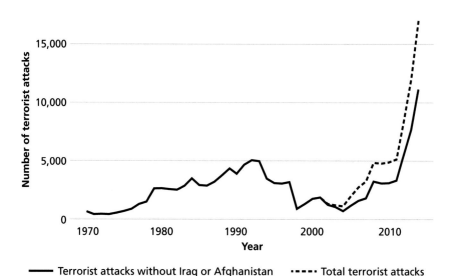

SOURCE: Megan Smith and Sean M. Seigler, "Terrorism Before and After 911: A More Dangerous World?" *Research & Politics*, October–December 2017, p. 2 (CC by 4.0).

about 1991, the approximate end of the Cold War, until 2003, the year that the U.S.-led coalition invaded Iraq. At that point, the frequency of terrorist attacks rose sharply in countries suffering ongoing conflicts, even though most of the attacks up until 2010 were not in Afghanistan or Iraq (as Figure 6.2 indicates). These figures reflect the spread of extremist violence in conflicts across the Muslim world. The locations of these conflicts correlate strongly with states in the highest categories of the Fragile States Index, suggesting once again that the democratization of violence, and thus incidents of terrorism, will continue at comparable rates over the next ten to 15 years. However, there are reasons to suspect that the rates will be even higher.

Groups carrying out dangerous transnational terrorist attacks often do not originate in the most fragile states, nor do they launch their attacks from these states. Furthermore, the targets of these attacks are often located in the most-developed nations. Stewart Patrick argues that states categorized as mid-range in the Index—those typically more

Figure 6.3
Terrorist Attacks in Conflict Countries and Nonconflict Countries, 1990–2015

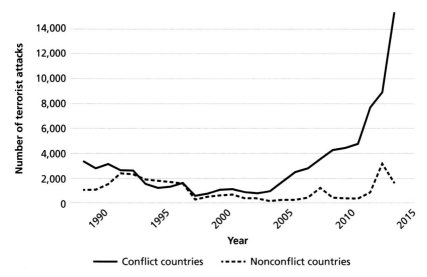

SOURCE: Smith and Seigler, 2017, p. 2 (CC by 4.0).

capable than the states most at risk but less capable than the most-developed nations—are actually the ones that provide the best launching pads for transnational terrorism.[9] This might be because these states have the infrastructure that terrorist groups need to organize their attacks—infrastructure that is often lacking or nonfunctional in the states most at risk—while lacking the degree of law enforcement oversight that more-developed states possess. Conversely, other analysts have argued that the highest-threat terrorist groups might arise in the most technologically advanced societies, as was illustrated in the case of Aum Shinrikyo in Japan. This could be particularly troubling if future advances in such fields as biotechnology provide opportunities for mass-casualty terrorism on scales not yet seen. In any case, past major attacks in New York, Madrid, Paris, Brussels, and other cities

---

[9] Stewart Patrick, *Weak Links: Fragile States, Global Threats, and International Security,* Oxford: Oxford University Press, 2011.

suggest that terrorist violence in the next ten to 15 years might not be limited to the states listed as most at risk in the Fragile States Index. This violence also might be more frequent or severe than the stability that the numbers in that index would suggest.

Third-Party State Involvement

Another reason that incidents of substate violence could occur more in the next ten to 15 years than trends in the Fragile States Index would suggest is because third-party states could become more involved in regional conflicts. As already mentioned, third-party state involvement was the source of much of the substate violence in the late Cold War era. That violence subsided when the Cold War's ideological competition ended and interstate conflict declined. The first decade of the post–Cold War era was a time of increased cooperation between permanent members of the United Nations Security Council that increased the effectiveness of mechanisms for conflict management, such as peace operations and international dispute mediation. Although an analysis of changing global relationships is beyond the scope of this report, if relations between the great powers were to deteriorate in the next ten to 15 years, the Security Council could become paralyzed, mechanisms for conflict management could break down, and states could increase their involvement in regional conflicts. That would likely result in democratization of violence at higher levels than trends in the Fragile States Index would suggest.[10]

Implications for the U.S. Air Force and the Future of Warfare

Assuming that the United States does not disavow its interests in promoting order and stability in the developing world, U.S. forces abroad

---

[10] For an analysis of several possible scenarios that could increase risks of interstate and intrastate war in the future, see Stephen Watts, Bryan Frederick, Jennifer Kavanagh, Angela O'Mahoney, Thomas S. Szayna, Matthew Lane, Alexander Stephenson, and Colin P. Clarke, *A More Peaceful World? Regional Conflict Trends and U.S. Defense Planning*, Santa Monica, Calif.: RAND Corporation, RR-1177-A, 2017, pp. 85–107.

will continue to be challenged by well-armed, radical substate groups. This could be particularly troublesome in Africa, the Middle East, and South Asia—the locations of most of the states in the top three most at-risk categories.[11] As a result, there will be a continuing need for the USAF to provide air, space, and cyber ISR to provide situational awareness and identify, track, and target dangerous individuals and groups. The USAF also will be called upon to support U.S. and friendly ground operations against substate groups and conduct manned and unmanned strike missions against selected targets.[12]

Given the ongoing demand for these operations, the USAF will need to continue to resource them while also preparing to combat higher-end adversaries. One possible solution under consideration is fielding a light attack aircraft to perform the strike and close air support missions in these operations and reserving platforms that are more technologically advanced for use in higher-end conflicts.[13] These efficiencies might relieve the strain on strike aircraft, but these operations will continue to impose an ongoing tax on the USAF and, particularly, its ISR and special operations communities.

---

[11] This assumes that state fragility has equally destabilizing effects in all of these regions, but post–Cold War conflict trends indicate that this might not be the case. They suggest that violence by radical substate groups will be greater in the Middle East and South Asia than in sub-Saharan Africa. Watts et al., 2017, pp. 41–47, 202–205.

[12] For more analysis, see Ochmanek et al., 2017, pp. 77–94.

[13] See Valerie Insinna, "The Light-Attack Aircraft Competition Will Be Down to Two Competitors," *Defense News*, August 6, 2018.

CHAPTER SEVEN

Trend 6: AI as a Class of Potentially Disruptive Technologies

Context: Developments in AI Are Emerging at a Sharply Accelerating Rate

Military applications of AI could significantly change the character of war in the next ten to 15 years. Researchers and developers in computer science and related fields have worked on building intelligent machines since the early 1950s, but the most dramatic advances have been made in the past couple of decades. Over the next decade and a half, rapid progress in the development of autonomous weapons, robotics, big data analysis, and decision-support systems using deep neural networks could revolutionize warfare. Unfortunately, U.S. forces will not have a monopoly on these technologies.

Historical Trend: Dramatic Advances Have Occurred in Computer Vision, Speech Recognition, Natural Language Processing, and Robotics

Many people attribute the birth of AI to Alan Turing's 1950 essay, "Computing Machinery and Intelligence," but the term *artificial intelligence* was first used as a title to a conference held at Dartmouth College in 1955, at which the organizers proposed that "every aspect of learning or any other feature of intelligence can in principle be so precisely described that a machine can be made to simulate it."[1] In the years since, progress in AI research has gone through visible cycles of boom, when expected advances kindled surges in funding, and bust, when those expectations failed to manifest, putting the field in disfavor with government and industrial patrons.[2] Perhaps the first milestone in the development of AI that captured widespread public attention was in 1997, when IBM's intelligent system, Big Blue, defeated then–world chess champion Gary Kasparov in a six-game match. Even more impressively, Google DeepMind's AlphaGo system defeated Lee Sedol, the world's top-ranked player of the Asian game of Go, four games to one in 2016.[3] Chess has 20 possible first moves per side and 10^{120} total possible board configurations; Go has 361 possible first moves per side and 10^{170} total possible board configurations, more than the total number of atoms in the universe.[4]

In the years since Big Blue's triumph, AI research has made dramatic advances in the fields of computer vision, speech recognition, natural language processing, and robotics. Efforts to develop computer vision began in the 1960s but made little headway until about a decade ago, when the application of convolutional neural networks enabled vision processing systems to "learn" by building models of objects based on observations of large collections of examples.[5] Recent progress has

---

[1] See A. M. Turing, "Computing Machinery and Intelligence," *Mind*, Vol. 59, No. 236, October 1950; J. McCarthy, M. L. Minsky, N. Rochester, and C. E. Shannon, "A Proposal for the Dartmouth Summer Research Project on Artificial Intelligence," August 31, 1955, reprinted in *AI Magazine*, Vol. 27, No. 4, 2006.

[2] Jerry Kaplan, *Artificial Intelligence*, Oxford: Oxford University Press, 2016, p. 16.

[3] "Google Achieves AI 'Breakthrough' by Beating Go Champion," BBC News, January 27, 2016.

[4] Danielle Muolo, "Why Go Is So Much Harder for AI to Beat Than Chess," *Business Insider*, March 10, 2016.

[5] A *convolutional neural network* is a class of deep neural network specialized for analyzing visual imagery. A deep neural network is a complex system of layered algorithms, the outputs of each layer constituting inputs for subsequent layers, inspired by the function of biological neural networks that make up animal brains. In convolutional neural networks, the connectivity pattern between artificial neurons resembles the organization of the animal visual cortex. See Kaplan, 2016, p. 54.

resulted in increasingly reliable facial recognition systems and emerging capabilities for analyzing video data. Speech recognition has been a more difficult problem in some ways, given the many complexities of language. However, the development of hidden Markov modeling—a statistical technique that can be applied to calculate probabilities regarding the meanings of patterns of sound—and the recent application of a deep learning method called *long short-term memory* have enabled advances leading to speech recognition systems now used in smartphones and other computer devices.[6] These advances and others allow people to interact with intelligent systems—i.e., to enter data, ask questions, and receive spoken or written responses—using natural language rather than computer code.

The most publicized advances in robotics have probably been in the field of self-driving vehicles, but robots are also being employed in a host of other areas, such as industrial assembly; entertainment; and operations in environments hostile to human life, such as outer space, areas of nuclear contamination, and combat. In military applications of AI, one of the latest capabilities to emerge is robotic swarming, large numbers of autonomous vehicles or weapons programmed with rules that, when applied in aggregate by the entire group, exhibit emergent behavior that makes them much more effective in combat than would be possible by the same number of devices under human control.[7]

---

[6]   Sepp Hockreiter and Jurgen Schmidhuber, "Long Short-Term Memory," *Neural Computation*, Vol. 9, No. 8, November 15, 1997.

[7]   Paul Scharre and Shawn Brimley, "20YY: The Future of Warfare," *War on the Rocks*, January 29, 2014; Kaplan, 2016, pp. 49–53; Paul Scharre, *Army of None: Autonomous Weapons and the Future of War*, New York: W. W. Norton, 2018, pp. 17–22.

Future Projection: Military Applications of AI Could Create Systems So Capable That They Change the Character of Warfare

Some experts maintain that advances in the next ten to 15 years will be even more dramatic, potentially changing the character of warfare.[8] For instance, the military forces of developed nations might increasingly employ autonomous weapons that can find, identify, track, target, and engage enemy forces without human operators taking part in the decision process. By making human interaction unnecessary, autonomous weapons will shorten the "observe-orient-decide-act (OODA) loop," enabling these forces to act and react more quickly than their enemies.[9] This could be particularly effective in the cyber domain, where autonomous programs will learn to analyze adversaries' offensive and defensive systems and change their own software to close gaps or exploit enemy vulnerabilities at speeds that human operators are unable to match.[10] In the physical world, autonomous weapons will be able to loiter in combat areas much longer than manned systems could, ever vigilant, collecting intelligence and striking targets as they appear.[11] These capabilities also will relieve human operators of many tasks that are dangerous or prone to human error due to boredom or fatigue.

AI will allow warfighters to bring "big data" to bear in the analysis of volumes of information that would be impossible for humans to process. Machine learning systems will employ advanced pattern recognition to these data, identifying enemy tactics and hidden targets, improving accuracy, and supporting command decisionmaking with

---

[8] Aaron Mehta, "AI Makes Mattis Question 'Fundamental' Beliefs About War," *C4ISRNET*, February 17, 2018. For a deeper discussion, see Robert H. Latiff, *Future War: Preparing for the New Global Battlefield*, New York: Alfred A. Knopf, 2017.

[9] Scharre, 2018, pp. 23–24; "Autonomous Weapons Are a Game-Changer," *The Economist*, January, 25, 2018.

[10] Scharre, 2018, pp. 222–227; Deepak Dutt, "2018: The Year of the AI-Powered Cyber Attack," *CSO*, January 10, 2018.

[11] Guia Marie Del Prado, "These Weapons Can Find Targets All by Themselves—and Researchers Are Terrified," *Business Insider*, July 30, 2015.

levels of speed and reliability not possible with human-only staffs.[12] Finally, by taking human decisionmaking out of the loop, intelligent systems could relieve commanders of emotionally tough decisions. Even if commanders choose not to delegate these tough decisions, AI could allow them to make these decisions with more confidence and, perhaps, a clearer conscience.[13]

These Capabilities Will Come with Serious Risks

By making weapons and decision-support systems more autonomous, AI will tighten the observe-orient-decide-act loop, resulting in quicker but not necessarily better decisions. Intelligent systems might not be able to distinguish between combatants and noncombatants as accurately as human warfighters can, and when there is uncertainty, autonomous weapons will decide whether to strike based on mathematical probabilities rather than human conscience.[14] Moreover, the quality of decisions made by AI might not always be reliable for other reasons. If the data behind the AI system are incomplete or biased, the quality of decisionmaking is degraded.[15] Adversaries might be able to corrupt the data or hack into the AI system itself.[16] Such vulnerabilities are frightening when systems are granted the autonomy to employ lethal force. On the other hand, not employing these systems with sufficient autonomy will also be risky if adversaries are doing so and gaining combat advantages from the speed and precision available from automated warfare.

Intelligent weapons and decision-support systems might not be sensitive to the subtle nuances of political tension, restraint, and brinkmanship in a crisis. They might not respond to deterrent threats or understand the concept of escalation management. They could cause

---

[12] Kaplan, 2016, pp. 117–118.

[13] For discussion of how intelligent systems might interact with humans in a variety of warfighting ethical dilemmas, see Latiff, 2017, pp. 91–121.

[14] Latiff, 2017, p. 117.

[15] Scott Fortmann-Roe, "Understanding the Bias-Variance Tradeoff," blog post, June 2012.

[16] Scharre, 2018, pp. 182–183, 246–247.

deterrence to fail or could strike at the wrong times, places, or levels of intensity, quickly escalating minor conflicts into major wars.[17] Furthermore, if both sides are employing autonomous systems, these systems might interact in a rapidly escalating fashion that AI researcher Paul Scharre describes as "flash war."[18]

The United States Will Not Have a Monopoly on These Capabilities

Former Secretary of Defense Chuck Hagel and others have advocated that the United States develop the military applications of AI to regain the qualitative advantage that it had over the conventional capabilities of potential adversaries during the Gulf War.[19] Unfortunately, the United States will not have a monopoly on these technologies because, unlike the development of stealth; precision-guidance; and command, control, communications, computer, and ISR capabilities during the 1970s and 1980s, the technologies that make up AI are being developed in the academic and commercial sectors of many countries.

The United States' closest near-peer competitors, China and Russia, are aggressively developing autonomous weapons and other military applications of AI. China, in particular, is investing heavily in developing autonomous vehicles in all domains (particularly air and ground operations), and automated systems for command-and-control, ISR processing, equipment design, and training.[20] Russia has devoted less resources to date and has concentrated largely on AI applications

---

[17] Elsa Kania, "Great Power Competition and the AI Revolution: A Range of Risks to Military and Strategic Stability," *LAWFARE*, September 19, 2017.

[18] The term *flash war* is fashioned after the term *flash crash*, which describes rapid, cascading drops in financial markets caused or exacerbated by high-speed electronic selling initiated by AI systems with algorithms programmed to sell shares when they detect rapid drops in prices. See Paul Scharre, "Flash War: Autonomous Weapons and Strategic Stability," briefing, Washington, D.C., Center for New American Security, undated. Also see Scharre, 2018, pp. 207–210.

[19] Hagel described this effort as the "Third Offset Strategy," a term that was later discarded by Secretary of Defense James Mattis. See Kathleen Hicks and Andrew Hunter, "What Will Replace the Third Offset? Lessons from Past Innovation Strategies," *Defense One*, March 17, 2017.

[20] Elsa Kania, "Beyond CFIUS: The Strategic Challenge of China's Rise in Artificial Intelligence," *LAWFARE*, June 20, 2017.

for electronic warfare, where Moscow feels Russia has a comparative advantage. However, Moscow announced plans in February 2018 to build a "technopolis" to concentrate scientific talent from multiple fields in one location and work on developing AI, robotics, and pattern-recognition technologies for military application.[21] Both countries are taking advantage of permissive privacy laws (and compliant citizens) to collect and fuse data from public, private, and social network sources to train their machine learning systems and maintain domestic security and control.[22]

Implications for the U.S. Air Force and the Future of Warfare

AI will likely change the character of military operations to some extent in all domains during the next ten to 15 years, and the United States cannot afford to allow any potential adversary to dominate this field. The capabilities this technology offers will enhance military missions at all levels of conflict. For instance, the USAF will benefit from autonomous standoff weapons when missions require penetrating denied airspace, and machine learning analysis of ISR data will assist in target identification and tracking. China and Russia are pressing ahead in the development of autonomous weapons even as they lobby the international community to ban them in efforts to tie the hands of the United States. Both countries hope their military applications of AI will offset the technological advantages that U.S. forces currently possess. For its own security, the United States must press ahead with its own developmental programs.

The risks that attend the proliferation of military applications of AI will be substantial. Autonomous weapons could attack the wrong

---

[21] President of Russia, "Presentation of Era Innovation Technopolis," Moscow: Kremlin, February 23, 2018; Samuel Bendett, "Russia Wants to Build a Whole City for Developing Deadly Weapons," *National Interest*, March 29, 2018.

[22] Agence France Presse/Jiji Press, "China Using Big Data and 'Predictive Policing' in Xinjiang Region to Round Up Perceived Threats: HRW," *Japan Times*, February 28, 2018; "Russia: Assault on Internet Freedom, Cyber Security," Human Rights Watch, April 30, 2018.

targets, and they could prosecute attacks in areas or at intensities that human judgment would consider inappropriate, triggering escalation. Even more seriously—at least, in the eyes of many citizens in the United States and elsewhere—the prospect of machines deciding to take human life and acting on those decisions without human intervention is morally repugnant. It could also violate the laws of armed conflict.

Therefore, as the United States develops various military applications of AI, DoD and its service components will need to educate the public on why these capabilities are so important. Such education needs to emphasize the nation's commitment to adhering to the highest ethical, moral, and legal standards in development and employment of these capabilities. The USAF should explain that the principal focus of its AI development efforts is on applications that offer high reward at lower risk—systems to assist in ISR analysis, logistics, and force protection—and not on the so-called killer robots that critics are so concerned about.

Ultimately, as the United States presses ahead in this field, U.S. leaders, system developers, and military practitioners will need to work together to determine what balance of human-machine teaming will maximize the benefits of autonomy while keeping within the boundaries of acceptable risk.

CHAPTER EIGHT

Conclusion: Understanding the Eroding "Competitive Military Advantage"

Given these trends in the size, quality, and character of U.S. conventional military forces in relation to those of potential adversaries, the United States will likely face serious challenges in the next ten to 15 years. Table 8.1 summarizes the findings of these trends and challenges.

As the table indicates, the risks of war over the next ten to 15 years will largely derive from perceptions of shifts in regional correlations of force. With U.S. conventional forces reduced in size, China—and, to a lesser extent, Russia—will narrow the qualitative gap and might calculate that the United States might lack sufficient capacity—in some cases, the capability—to respond effectively. Such wars, if they occur, will be multidomain conflicts fought under an ever-present risk of nuclear escalation.

China and Russia, however, likely will prefer to achieve their objectives "on the cheap"—i.e., with the least cost in international reproach and the lowest risk of provoking military conflict with the United States. Instead, both will likely ramp up their use of gray-zone tactics. Countering these strategies will require the United States to persistently confront such aggressive tactics and to be prepared to fight at multiple levels of conflict, from subconventional through conventional.

Iran and North Korea do not have—and are unlikely to develop—capabilities to match those of the United States and its regional allies. However, they will have selected asymmetric capabilities to deter U.S.

Table 8.1
Summary of Findings

Trend	Who Will Fight	How the United States Will Fight	Where the United States Will Fight	Why the United States Will Fight
Decreasing U.S. conventional force size		Multidomain under nuclear shadow with some amount of artificial intelligence (AI)		Regional aggressor calculates that the United States lacks capacity to respond effectively in a given theater because of its other global commitments
Increasing modernization and professionalization of near-peer forces	China or Russia vs. United States and select allies or partners	Multidomain under nuclear shadow with some amount of AI	East China Sea, Taiwan, South China Sea, Baltics, or elsewhere on peripheries	China or Russia calculates that it can deny the United States sufficient access to defeat effort to change territorial status quo
Development of asymmetric strategies by second-tier powers	Iran or North Korea vs. United States, allies, and partners	Neutralize selective capabilities, then destroy large but less-sophisticated forces	Middle East or Korean peninsula	Iranian machinations/North Korean provocations lead to war
Potential adversaries' increasing use of "gray zone" tactics	Quasi-military or covert state forces, nonstate actors	Subconventional or hybrid, potentially escalating to conventional	In disputed territories and areas where state control is weak	States victimized by covert or proxy forces will need support
Weakening of the state's monopoly on violence	Heavily armed individuals and groups	Subconventional or hybrid	Areas of failed or weak state control—Africa, Middle East, South Asia	States unable to restrain heavily armed individuals and groups will need support
AI as a class of potentially disruptive technologies	Highly advanced states	Multidomain under nuclear shadow with autonomous weapons		Regional aggressor believes its AI capabilities are sufficient to change the status quo

intervention and the ability to employ gray-zone tactics in pursuit of their regional objectives. If their aggressive strategies ultimately lead to war, U.S. forces will need to find ways to neutralize those asymmetric capabilities and destroy substantial portions of those adversaries' large but less-sophisticated forces.

The use of substate actors as proxy fighters in gray-zone strategies will continue weakening the state's monopoly on violence in many areas of the world. As aggressive states arm individuals and groups in regions they seek to destabilize or annex, the weaker states will have difficulty containing the violence that results and likely will turn to the United States for support. Given U.S. interests in maintaining stability and the territorial status quo in many of these regions, the United States will need devote resources to these missions even as it is trying to restore its conventional capabilities for great-power competition.

Developments in military applications of AI might help in both of these arenas, providing advanced systems that restore U.S. qualitative advantages in conventional warfare and providing capabilities to process ISR data in ways that enable U.S. forces to identify and target substate adversaries more effectively. As the nation's military service with the preponderance of ISR, rapid deployment, and deep strike capabilities, the USAF will be on the leading edge of military applications of AI. However, these capabilities come with serious risks that will need to be managed, and the United States will not have a monopoly on access to them. Barring strong and verifiable arms control agreements limiting the development or employment of these technologies—which appears highly unlikely at this point—the United States cannot afford to not develop them while China and Russia are pursuing them so aggressively. U.S. leaders will need to find ways to maximize the benefits they offer while mitigating the inevitable risks.

Taken together, these six trends give new meaning to what the *National Defense Strategy* describes as the growth of "interstate strategic competition" and the United States' "eroding" competitive military advantage. It is not so much that the United States risks being replaced wholesale as the dominant global military power by any single adversary, at least in the near term (although this might be a concern in China's case over the longer haul). More, it is that the United States risks needing to confront so many different types of threats simultaneously that it cannot respond to any of them effectively.[1] As noted, each trend—high-end conflict with China or Russia, asymmetric conflict with Iran or North Korea, gray-zone conflict with all of the above, and the continued threat of terrorism—pushes the joint force and the USAF in somewhat different directions and demands a somewhat different suite of capabilities in response.[2] If the United States could field a larger force with elements tailored to each type of challenge, then this diversification of threats might not be an issue. As noted in the first trend, however, the overall size of the U.S. military has declined since its last major period of strategic competition and is unlikely to recover anytime soon. Nor can the United States hope for a technological panacea to solve this challenge. As noted in the last trend, the United States is unlikely to have a monopoly over potentially game-changing technologies, such as AI.

For the USAF and the joint force, then, erosion of the U.S. competitive military advantage will force harder choices about where to allocate a finite number of resources and demand that the United States take even greater risks in 2030 than it does now—and much greater risks than it took after the Cold War. Perhaps, this is what *National Defense Strategy* means by "we are emerging from a period of strategic atrophy."[3] By 2030, strategic choices will have even greater consequences, and trying to do it all might no longer be an option.

---

[1]   DoD, 2018, p. 1.

[2]   As the war in Syria has illustrated, such divergent demands could be placed on U.S. forces both globally and in a single campaign.

[3]   DoD, 2018, p. 1.

References

Adams, Karen Ruth, "Attack and Conquer? International Anarchy and the Offense-Defense-Deterrence Balance," *International Security*, Vol. 28, No. 3, Winter 2003–2004, pp. 45–83.

Agence France Presse/Jiji Press, "China Using Big Data and 'Predictive Policing' in Xinjiang Region to Round Up Perceived Threats: HRW," *Japan Times*, February 28, 2018.

Altosaar, Aimar, "Ida-Viru County and Russia," *Maailma Vaade*, No. 24, March 5, 2018. As of May 23, 2018:
http://www.maailmavaade.ee/nr24-en/ida-viru-county-and-russia

Arango, Tim, "Iran Dominates in Iraq After the U.S. 'Handed the Country Over,'" *New York Times*, July 15, 2017. As of May 21, 2018:
https://www.nytimes.com/2017/07/15/world/middleeast/iran-iraq-iranian-power.html

Associated Press, "Iran Deploys Air Defense System Around Fordo Nuclear Site," *New York Times*, August 29, 2016. As of May 17, 2018:
https://www.nytimes.com/2016/08/30/world/middleeast/iran-missiles-fordo-s300.html?_r=0

Atherton, Kelsey D., "Don't Believe the Hype About Russia's Hypersonic Missile," *Popular Science*, June 18, 2017. As of August 6, 2018:
https://www.popsci.com/hype-russia-hypersonic-missile

"Autonomous Weapons Are a Game-Changer," *The Economist*, January, 25, 2018. As of May 30, 2018:
https://www.economist.com/special-report/2018/01/25/autonomous-weapons-are-a-game-changer

Benari, Elad, "Pentagon: Iran Has Deployed the S-300 System," *Arutz Sheva*, March 8, 2018. As of May 17, 2018:
http://www.israelnationalnews.com/News/News.aspx/242867

Bendett, Samuel, "Russia Wants to Build a Whole City for Developing Deadly Weapons," *National Interest*, March 29, 2018. As of May 30, 2018:
http://nationalinterest.org/blog/the-buzz/russia-wants-build-whole-city-developing-deadly-weapons-25121

Bialik, Kristen, "U.S. Active-Duty Military Presence Overseas Is at Its Smallest in Decades," Pew Research Center, August 22, 2017. As of December 31, 2018:
http://www.pewresearch.org/fact-tank/2017/08/22/u-s-active-duty-military-presence-overseas-is-at-its-smallest-in-decades/

Björnehed, Emma, "Narcoterrorism: The Merger of the War on Drugs and the War on Terrorism," *Global Crime*, Vol. 6, No. 3, November 2004, pp. 305–324. As of May 25, 2018:
https://www.diplomatie.gouv.fr/IMG/pdf/drogue-terreur.pdf

Boston, Scott, Michael Johnson, Nathan Beauchamp-Mustafaga, and Yvonne K. Crane, *Assessing the Conventional Force Imbalance in Europe: Implications for Countering Russian Local Superiority*, Santa Monica, Calif.: RAND Corporation, RR-2402, 2018. As of August 23, 2018:
https://www.rand.org/pubs/research_reports/RR2402.html

Bryce-Rogers, Athena, "Russian Military Reform in the Aftermath of the 2008 Russia-Georgian War," *Demokratizatsiya: The Journal of Post-Soviet Democratization*, Vol. 2, No. 3, 2013, pp. 339–368.

Bucala, Paul, and Frederick W. Kagan, *Iran's Evolving Way of War: How the IRGC Fights in Syria*, Washington, D.C.: Critical Threats Project, March 15, 2016. As of May 21, 2018:
https://www.criticalthreats.org/analysis/irans-evolving-way-of-war-how-the-irgc-fights-in-syria

Bureau of Counterterrorism and Countering Violent Extremism, *Country Reports on Terrorism 2015*, Washington, D.C.: U.S. Department of State, June 2016. As of February 23, 2017:
https://www.state.gov/documents/organization/272488.pdf

Central Intelligence Agency, *International and Transnational Terrorism: Diagnosis and Prognosis*, Washington, D.C., PR 76 10030, April 1976. As of December 11, 2018:
https://www.cia.gov/library/readingroom/docs/DOC_0000658249.pdf

Chansoria, Monika, "China's Military Doctrine and Strategy: Continuity with Change," *CLAWS Journal*, winter 2009, pp. 94–117. As of May 15, 2018:
http://www.claws.in/images/journals_doc/1399528913Monika%20Chansoria%20CJ%20Winter%202009.pdf

Chelule, Esther, "Proliferation of Small Arms and Light Weapons: Challenge to Development, Peace and Security in Africa," *IOSR Journal of Humanities and Social Science*, Vol. 19, No. 5, May 2014, pp. 80–87.

Choe San-Hun, "Reunification with North Korea Unappealing for Younger South Koreans," *The Star*, January 28, 2018. As of May 21, 2018:
https://www.thestar.com/news/world/2018/01/28/reunification-with-north-korea-unappealing-for-young-south-koreans.html

Clarke, Hilary, and Shirzad Bozorgmehr, "Iran Unveils New Long-Range Ballistic Missile," CNN, September 23, 2017. As of May 17, 2018:
https://www.cnn.com/2017/09/23/middleeast/iran-ballistic-missile/index.html

Cohen, Raphael S., *The History and Politics of Defense Reviews*, Santa Monica, Calif.: RAND Corporation, RR-2278-AF, 2018. As of December 31, 2018:
https://www.rand.org/pubs/research_reports/RR2278.html

Cohen, Raphael S., Nathan Chandler, Shira Efron, Bryan Frederick, Eugeniu Han, Kurt Klein, Forrest E. Morgan, Ashley L. Rhoades, Howard J. Shatz, and Yuliya Shokh, *The Future of Warfare in 2030: Project Overview and Conclusions*, Santa Monica, Calif.: RAND Corporation, RR-2849/1-AF, 2020. As of May 2020:
https://www.rand.org/pubs/research_reports/RR2849z1.html

Cohen, Raphael S., Eugeniu Han, and Ashley Rhoades, *Geopolitical Trends and the Future of Warfare: The Changing Global Environment and Its Implications for the U.S. Air Force*, Santa Monica, Calif.: RAND Corporation, RR-2849/2, 2020. As of May 2020:
https://www.rand.org/pubs/research_reports/RR2849z2.html

Cohen, Raphael S., and Andrew Radin, *Russian Hostile Measures*, Santa Monica, Calif.: RAND Corporation, RR-1793-A, 2019. As of March 3, 2019:
https://www.rand.org/pubs/research_reports/RR1793.html

Colitti, Gianpaulo, "China Unveils Its New Hypervelocity Missile Programme," *UK Defence Journal*, June 13, 2017. As of August 6, 2018:
https://ukdefencejournal.org.uk/
china-unveils-new-hypervelocity-missile-programme/

Danczuk, Josef, "The Global Spread of Arms: The Link Between State Collapse, Small Arms Proliferation, and Global Conflict," *Military Review*, Vol. 96, No. 5, September–October 2016.

de Jomini, Antoine Henri, *The Art of War: A New Edition with Appendices and Maps*, trans. G. H. Mendell and W. P. Craighill, Philadelphia, Pa.: J. B. Lippincott & Co., 1862, reprint in Westport, Conn.: Greenwood Press, undated.

Del Prado, Guia Marie, "These Weapons Can Find Targets All by Themselves—and Researchers Are Terrified," *Business Insider*, July 30, 2015. As of May 30, 2018:
http://www.businessinsider.com/
which-artificially-intelligent-semi-autonomous-weapons-exist-2015-7

DoD—*See* U.S. Department of Defense.

Dutt, Deepak, "2018: The Year of the AI-Powered Cyber Attack," CSO, January 10, 2018. As of May 30, 2018:
https://www.csoonline.com/article/3246196/cyberwarfare/2018-the-year-of-the-ai-powered-cyberattack.html

Edelman, Eric, and Gary Roughhead, *Providing for the Common Defense: The Assessment and Recommendations of the National Defense Strategy Commission*, Washington, D.C.: U.S. Institute of Peace, 2018.

Efron, Shira, Kurt Klein, Raphael S. Cohen, *Environment, Geography and the Future of Warfare: The Changing Global Environment and Its Implications for the U.S. Air Force*, Santa Monica, Calif.: RAND Corporation, RR-2849/5-AF, 2020. As of May 2020:
https://www.rand.org/pubs/research_reports/RR2849z5.html

Estonian Foreign Intelligence Service, *International Security and Estonia 2018*, Tallin, Estonia: Ministry of Defence, 2018. As of May 23, 2018:
https://www.valisluureamet.ee/pdf/raport-2018-ENG-web.pdf

Feleke, Bethlehem, "China Tests Bombers on South China Sea Island," CNN, May 21, 2018. As of May 21, 2018:
https://www.cnn.com/2018/05/20/asia/south-china-sea-bombers-islands-intl/index.html

Fortmann-Roe, Scott, "Understanding the Bias-Variance Tradeoff," blog post, June 2012. As of May 30, 2018:
http://scott.fortmann-roe.com/docs/BiasVariance.html

Frederick, Bryan, and Nathan Chandler, *Restraint and the Future of Warfare: The Changing Global Environment and Its Implications for the U.S. Air Force*, Santa Monica, Calif.: RAND Corporation, RR-2849/6-AF, 2020. As of May 2020:
https://www.rand.org/pubs/research_reports/RR2849z6.html

Fund for Peace, Fragile States Index data sets, 2006–2018. As of May 25, 2018:
http://fundforpeace.org/fsi/

Gady, Franz-Stefan, "Iran, Russia Inching Closer to Su-30 Fighter Jet Deal," *The Diplomat*, December 1, 2016. As of December 10, 2018:
https://thediplomat.com/tag/iran-russia-su-30-co-production/

———, "Iran: Russian-Made S-300 Air Defense Missile Systems Placed on 'Combat Duty,'" *The Diplomat*, July 11, 2017. As of May 17, 2018:
https://thediplomat.com/2017/07/iran-russian-made-s-300-air-defense-missile-systems-placed-on-combat-duty/

Gerson, Michael S., "Conventional Deterrence in the Second Nuclear Age," *Parameters*, Vol. 39, No. 3, Autumn 2009, pp. 32–48.

Giles, Keir, *Assessing Russia's Reorganized and Rearmed Military*, Washington, D.C.: Carnegie Endowment for World Peace, task force white paper, May 3, 2017. As of May 15, 2018:
http://carnegieendowment.org/2017/05/03/
assessing-russia-s-reorganized-and-rearmed-military-pub-69853

Goble, Paul, "Experts: Estonia Has Successfully Integrated Nearly 90% of Its Ethnic Russians," *Estonian World*, March 1, 2018. As of May 23, 2018:
http://estonianworld.com/security/
experts-estonia-successfully-integrated-nearly-90-ethnic-russians/

"Google Achieves AI 'Breakthrough' by Beating Go Champion," BBC News, January 27, 2016. As of June 29, 2018:
https://www.bbc.com/news/technology-35420579

Heginbotham, Eric, Michael Nixon, Forrest E. Morgan, Jacob L. Heim, Jeff Hagen, Sheng Li, Jeffrey Engstrom, Martin C. Libicki, Paul DeLuca, David A. Shlapak, David R. Frelinger, Burgess Laird, Kyle Brady, and Lyle J. Morris, *The U.S.-China Military Scorecard: Forces, Geography, and the Evolving Balance of Power, 1996–2017*, Santa Monica, Calif.: RAND Corporation, RR-392-AF, 2015. As of June 20, 2018:
https://www.rand.org/pubs/research_reports/RR392.html

Herspring, Dale, "Russian Military Reform and Anatoly Serdyukov," *Problems of Post-Communism*, Vol. 55, No. 6, November/December 2008, pp. 20–32. As of May 15, 2018:
https://www.tandfonline.com/doi/pdf/10.2753/PPC1075-8216550602

Hicks, Kathleen, and Andrew Hunter, "What Will Replace the Third Offset? Lessons from Past Innovation Strategies," *Defense One*, March 17, 2017. As of May 30, 2018:
https://www.defenseone.com/ideas/2017/03/
what-will-replace-third-offset-lessons-past-innovation-strategies/136260/

Hockreiter, Sepp, and Jurgen Schmidhuber, "Long Short-Term Memory," *Neural Computation*, Vol. 9, No. 8, November 15, 1997, pp. 1735–1780.

Huth, Paul, and Bruce Russett, "What Makes Deterrence Work? Cases from 1900 to 1980," *World Politics*, Vol. 36, No. 4, 1984, pp. 496–526.

IISS—*See* International Institute for Strategic Studies.

Insinna, Valerie, "The Light-Attack Aircraft Competition Will Be Down to Two Competitors," *Defense News*, August 6, 2018. As of August 24, 2018:
https://www.defensenews.com/air/2018/08/06/
the-light-attack-aircraft-competition-will-be-down-to-two-competitors/

International Institute for Strategic Studies, "The United States," *The Military Balance*, Vols. 90–103, 1990–2003. As of June 28, 2018:
https://www.tandfonline.com/loi/tmib20

————, "North America," *The Military Balance*, Vols. 104–118, 2004–2018. As of June 28, 2018:
https://www.tandfonline.com/loi/tmib20

————, "Asia," *The Military Balance*, Vols. 117–118, 2017–2018. As of May 13, 2018:
https://www.tandfonline.com/loi/tmib20

————, "Russia and Eurasia," *The Military Balance*, Vols. 117–118, 2017–2018. As of May 13, 2018:
https://www.tandfonline.com/loi/tmib20

————, "Middle East and North Africa," *The Military Balance*, Vol. 118, 2018. As of May 13, 2018:
https://www.tandfonline.com/loi/tmib20

Jalabi, Raya, and Michael Gregory, "Cleric Moqtada al-Sadr's Block Wins Iraqi Election," Reuters, May 18, 2018. As of May 21, 2018:
https://www.reuters.com/article/us-iraq-election-results/
cleric-moqtada-al-sadrs-bloc-wins-iraq-election-idUSKCN1IJ2X0

Johnson, Jesse, "China Confirms Deployment of Fighters to South China Sea Island for the First Time," *Japan Times*, December 2, 2017. As of December 10, 2018:
https://www.japantimes.co.jp/news/2017/12/02/asia-pacific/
china-confirms-deployment-fighters-south-china-sea-island-first-time/

Kania, Elsa, "Beyond CFIUS: The Strategic Challenge of China's Rise in Artificial Intelligence," *LAWFARE*, June 20, 2017. As of May 30, 2018:
https://www.lawfareblog.com/
beyond-cfius-strategic-challenge-chinas-rise-artificial-intelligence

————, "Great Power Competition and the AI Revolution: A Range of Risks to Military and Strategic Stability," *LAWFARE*, September 19, 2017. As of May 30, 2018:
https://www.lawfareblog.com/great-power-competition-and-ai-revolution-range-
risks-military-and-strategic-stability

Kaplan, Jerry, *Artificial Intelligence*, Oxford: Oxford University Press, 2016.

Kelly, Terrence K., David C. Gompert, and Duncan Long, *Smarter Power, Stronger Partners*, Volume I, *Exploiting U.S. Advantages to Prevent Aggression*, Santa Monica, Calif.: RAND Corporation, RR-1359-A, 2016. As of February 18, 2019:
https://www.rand.org/pubs/research_reports/RR1359.html

Kfir, Isaac, "Iraq as a 'Client State' of Iran," *The Strategist*, March 7, 2018. As of May 21, 2018:
https://www.aspistrategist.org.au/iraq-client-state-iran/

Kim, Jack, "North Korea Mounts Long-Running Hack of South Korea Computers, Says Seoul," Reuters, June 13, 2016. As of May 21, 2018: https://www.reuters.com/article/ us-northkorea-southkorea-cyber-idUSKCN0YZ0BE

Klare, Michael T., "The Deadly Connection: Paramilitary Bands, Small Arms Diffusion, and State Failure," in Robert I. Rotberg, ed., *When States Fail: Causes and Consequences*, Princeton, N.J.: Princeton University Press, 2003, pp. 116–134.

Kosnik, Matthew, "Russia's Military Reform: Putin's Last Card," *Journal of Military and Strategic Studies*, Vol. 17, No. 1, 2016, pp. 144–161.

Latiff, Robert H., *Future War: Preparing for the New Global Battlefield*, New York: Alfred A. Knopf, 2017.

Luhn, Alec, "Moscow Threatens Sanctions Against Latvia over Removal of Russian from Secondary Schools," *The Telegraph*, April 3, 2018. As of May 23, 2018: https://www.telegraph.co.uk/news/2018/04/03/ moscow-threatens-sanctions-against-latvia-removal-russian-secondary/

"Majority of South Koreans Feel That North Korean Attitude Is Changing," *Hankoreh*, March 18, 2018. As of May 21, 2018: http://english.hani.co.kr/arti/english_edition/e_national/836587.html

Majumdar, Dave, "Could Iran Sink a U.S. Navy Aircraft Carrier?" *National Interest*, December 30, 2015. As of May 17, 2018: http://nationalinterest.org/blog/the-buzz/ could-iran-sink-us-navy-aircraft-carrier-14767

———, "5 North Korean Weapons South Korea Should Fear," *National Interest*, January 6, 2016. As of May 17, 2018: http://nationalinterest.org/ feature/5-north-korean-weapons-south-korea-should-fear-14825

Martinson, Ryan D., "The Arming of China's Maritime Frontier," *China Maritime Report*, No. 2, June 2017. As of May 19, 2018: https://daisukybiendong.files.wordpress.com/2017/09/ryan-d-martinson-2017-the-arming-of-china_s-maritime-frontier-signed.pdf

McCarthy, J., M. L. Minsky, N. Rochester, and C. E. Shannon, "A Proposal for the Dartmouth Summer Research Project on Artificial Intelligence," August 31, 1955, reprinted in *AI Magazine*, Vol. 27, No. 4, 2006. As of May 27, 2018: https://www.aaai.org/ojs/index.php/aimagazine/article/download/1904/1802

McDermott, Roger, "Russia's Conventional Armed Forces and the Georgian War," *Parameters*, Vol. 39, No. 1, Spring 2009, pp. 65–80.

Mearsheimer, John J., *Conventional Deterrence*, Ithaca, N.Y.: Cornell University Press, 1983.

Mehta, Aaron, "AI Makes Mattis Question 'Fundamental' Beliefs About War," *C4ISRNET*, February 17, 2018. As of May 30, 2018:
https://www.c4isrnet.com/intel-geoint/2018/02/17/
ai-makes-mattis-question-fundamental-beliefs-about-war/

Messner, J. J., Nate Haken, Patricia Taft, Ignatius Onyekwere, Hannah Blyth, Charles Fiertz, Christina Murphy, Amanda Quinn, and McKenzie Horwitz, *2018 Fragile States Index*, Washington, D.C.: Fund for Peace, 2018. As of May 25, 2018:
http://fundforpeace.org/fsi/2018/04/24/fragile-states-index-2018-annual-report/

Miller, Christopher, "Anxious Ukraine Risks Escalation in 'Creeping Offensive,'" Radio Free Europe/Radio Liberty, January 30, 2017. As of February 23, 2017:
https://www.rferl.org/a/ukraine-russia-creeping-offensive-escalation-fighting/28268104.html

Mizokami, Kyle, "Could North Korea Annihilate Seoul with Its Artillery?" *National Interest*, April 25, 2017. As of May 17, 2018:
http://nationalinterest.org/blog/the-buzz/
could-north-korea-annihilate-seoul-its-artillery-20345?page=show

Monteiro, Nuno P., "Rest Unassured: Why Unipolarity Has Not Been Peaceful," *International Security*, Vol. 36, No. 3, Winter 2011–2012, pp. 9–40.

Muolo, Danielle, "Why Go Is So Much Harder for AI to Beat Than Chess," *Business Insider*, March 10, 2016. As of May 27, 2018:
http://www.businessinsider.com/
why-google-ai-game-go-is-harder-than-chess-2016-3

Musah, Abdel-Fatau, "Privatization of Security, Arms Proliferation, and the Process of State Collapse in Africa," *Development and Change*, Vol. 33, No. 5, 2002, pp. 911–933. As of May 25, 2018:
https://onlinelibrary.wiley.com/doi/pdf/10.1111/1467-7660.t01-1-00254

Naval History and Heritage Command, "U.S. Navy Active Ship Force Levels, 2000–2006," November 17, 2017. As of May 5, 2018:
https://www.history.navy.mil/research/histories/ship-histories/us-ship-force-levels.html#2000

Nichol, Jim, *Russian Military Reform and Defense Policy*, Washington, D.C.: Congressional Research Service, R42006, August 24, 2011. As of May 15, 2018:
https://fas.org/sgp/crs/row/R42006.pdf

Nixon, Richard, "Save the Peace Dividend," *New York Times*, November 19, 1992.

"N. Korea Likely Hacked S. Korea Cyber Command: Military," Yonhap News, December 6, 2016. As of May 21, 2018:
http://english.yonhapnews.co.kr/news/2016/12/05/0200000000
AEN20161205010451315.html

"North Korea Hacks South's Military Cyber Command," BBC News, December 6, 2016. As of May 21, 2018:
http://www.bbc.com/news/world-asia-38219009

"North Korea: 'No Apology' for S Korea Cheonan Sinking," BBC News, March 24, 2015. As of May 21, 2018:
http://www.bbc.com/news/world-asia-32013750

Ochmanek, David, *Restoring U.S. Power Projection Capabilities: Responding to the 2018 National Defense Strategy*, Santa Monica, Calif.: RAND Corporation, PE-260-AF, 2018. As of August 22, 2018:
https://www.rand.org/pubs/perspectives/PE260.html

Ochmanek, David, Peter A. Wilson, Brenna Allen, John Speed Meyers, and Carter C. Price, *U.S. Military Capabilities and Forces for a Dangerous World: Rethinking the U.S. Approach to Force Planning*, Santa Monica, Calif.: RAND Corporation, RR-1782-1-RC, 2017. As of July 26, 2018:
https://www.rand.org/pubs/research_reports/RR1782-1.html

Office of the Undersecretary of Defense (Comptroller)/Chief Financial Officer, *Defense Budget Overview: United States Department of Defense Fiscal Year 2019 Budget Request*, Washington, D.C.: U.S. Department of Defense, February 2018a. As of May 11, 2018:
https://dod.defense.gov/Portals/1/Documents/pubs/FY2019-Budget-Request-Overview-Book.pdf

———, *Fiscal Year 2019 Budget Request*, Washington, D.C.: U.S. Department of Defense, February 2018b. As of May 11, 2018:
https://www.defense.gov/News/News-Releases/News-Release-View/Article/1438798/dod-releases-fiscal-year-2019-budget-proposal/

———, *National Defense Budget Estimates for FY 2019*, Washington, D.C.: U.S. Department of Defense, April 2018c.

O'Mahony, Angela, Miranda Priebe, Bryan Frederick, Jennifer Kavanagh, Matthew Lane, Trevor Johnston, Thomas S. Szayna, Jakub P. Hlávka, Stephen Watts, and Matthew Povlock, *U.S. Presence and the Incidence of Conflict*, Santa Monica, Calif.: RAND Corporation, RR-1906-A, 2018. As of December 31, 2018:
https://www.rand.org/pubs/research_reports/RR1906.html

Orttung, Robert, and Christopher Walker, "Putin's Frozen Conflicts," *Foreign Policy*, February 13, 2015. As of May 23, 2018:
http://foreignpolicy.com/2015/02/13/putins-frozen-conflicts/

Oxenstierna, Susanna, "Russian Defence Spending and the Economic Decline," *Journal of Eurasian Studies*, Vol. 7, No. 1, January 2016, pp. 60–70. As of May 15, 2018:
https://www.sciencedirect.com/science/article/pii/S1879366515000287

Patrick, Stewart, *Weak Links: Fragile States, Global Threats, and International Security*, Oxford: Oxford University Press, 2011.

Pearson, James, and Ju-Min Park, "The War That Never Ends Between the Koreas," Reuters, June 16, 2014. As of May 21, 2018:
https://www.reuters.com/article/
us-northkorea-islands-insight-idUSKBN0ES00720140617

Petersen, Michael, "The Perils of Conventional Deterrence by Punishment," *War on the Rocks*, November 11, 2006. As of May 5, 2018:
https://warontherocks.com/2016/11/
the-perils-of-conventional-deterrence-by-punishment/

Pettyjohn, Stacie L., *U.S. Global Defense Posture, 1783–2011*, Santa Monica, Calif.: RAND Corporation, MG-1244-AF, 2011. As of December 31, 2018:
https://www.rand.org/pubs/monographs/MG1244.html

Prentice, Alexandra, "Ukraine, Allies Fear Escalation After Russia Exits Ceasefire Group," Reuters, December 20, 2017. As of May 23, 2018:
https://www.reuters.com/article/us-ukraine-crisis-conflict-jccc/
ukraine-allies-fear-escalation-after-russia-exits-ceasefire-group-idUSKBN1EE1X2

President of Russia, "Presentation of Era Innovation Technopolis," Moscow: Kremlin, February 23, 2018. As of May 30, 2018:
http://en.kremlin.ru/events/president/news/56923

Public Law 115-96, Third Continuing Appropriations for Fiscal Year 2018, Division B, Missile Defense, Title I, Missile Defeat and Defense Enhancements, December 22, 2017. As of February 15, 2019:
https://www.congress.gov/115/plaws/publ96/PLAW-115publ96.pdf

Rai, Manish, "Iraq Is a Client State of Iran," *International Policy Digest*, November 9, 2017.

Reisinger, Heidi, and Aleksandr Golts, *Russia's Hybrid Warfare: Waging War Below the Radar of Traditional Collective Defence*, Rome: NATO Defense College, Research Paper No. 105, November 2014. As of February 17, 2017:
https://www.files.ethz.ch/isn/185744/rp_105.pdf

Rhodes, Edward, "Conventional Deterrence," *Comparative Strategy*, Vol. 19, No. 3, 2000, pp. 221–253.

Rid, Thomas, "Cyber War Will Not Take Place," *Journal of Strategic Studies*, Vol. 35, No. 1, February 2012, pp. 5–32.

Roberts, Brad, *The Case for U.S. Nuclear Weapons in the 21st Century*, Stanford, Calif.: Stanford University Press, 2016.

Robinson, Linda, Todd C. Helmus, Raphael S. Cohen, Alireza Nader, Andrew Radin, Madeline Magnuson, and Katya Migacheva, *Modern Political Warfare: Current Practices and Possible Responses*, Santa Monica, Calif.: RAND Corporation, RR-1772-A, 2017. As of February 18, 2019:
https://www.rand.org/pubs/research_reports/RR1772.html

Roffey, Roger, "Russian Science and Technology Is Still Having Problems—Implications for Defense Research," *Journal of Slavic Military Studies*, Vol. 26, No. 2, 2013, pp. 162–188. As of May 16, 2018:
https://www.tandfonline.com/doi/abs/10.1080/13518046.2013.779849

Ross, Eleanor, "North Korea Military: What to Know About Life as a Soldier in Kim Jong Un's Army," *Newsweek*, June 21, 2017. As of May 17, 2018:
http://www.newsweek.com/
soldiers-life-north-korean-army-marked-hunger-and-defections-are-rising-627596

"Russia: Assault on Internet Freedom, Cyber Security," Human Rights Watch, April 30, 2018. As of June 29, 2018:
https://www.hrw.org/news/2018/04/30/
russia-assault-internet-freedom-cybersecurity

"Russia 'Test-Fires Hypersonic Kinzal Missile,'" BBC News, March 11, 2018. As of August 6, 2018:
https://www.bbc.com/news/world-europe-43362213

Ryall, Julian, "North Korea Waging 'Cyber Warfare' Against South by Spreading Malicious Rumours," *Telegraph*, October 25, 2016. As of May 21, 2018:
https://www.telegraph.co.uk/news/2016/10/25/
north-korea-waging-cyber-warfare-against-south-by-spreading-mali/

Scharre, Paul, "Flash War: Autonomous Weapons and Strategic Stability," briefing, Washington, D.C., Center for New American Security, undated. As of May 30, 2018:
http://www.unidir.ch/files/conferences/pdfs/-en-1-1113.pdf

———, *Army of None: Autonomous Weapons and the Future of War*, New York: W. W. Norton, 2018.

Scharre, Paul, and Shawn Brimley, "20YY: The Future of Warfare," *War on the Rocks*, January 29, 2014. As of May 30, 2018:
https://warontherocks.com/2014/01/20yy-the-future-of-warfare/

Schelling, Thomas C., *Arms and Influence*, New Haven, Conn.: Yale University Press, 1966.

Schnaubelt, Christopher M., Craig A. Bond, Frank Camm, Joshua Klimas, Beth E. Lachman, Laurie L. McDonald, Judith D. Mele, Paul Ng, Meagan L. Smith, Cole Sutera, and Christopher Skeels, *The Army's Local Economic Effects*, Santa Monica, Calif.: RAND Corporation, RR-1119-A, 2015. As of December 31, 2018:
https://www.rand.org/pubs/research_reports/RR1119.html

Scobell, Andrew, and John M. Sanford, *North Korea's Military Threat: Pyongyang's Conventional Forces, Weapons of Mass Destruction, and Ballistic Missiles*, Carlisle, Pa.: Strategic Studies Institute, April 2007. As of May 17, 2018:
https://ssi.armywarcollege.edu/pdffiles/PUB771.pdf

Seidel, Jamie, "Hypervelocity Missile Breakthrough Makes China the World Leader in New Weaponry," news.com.au, December 31, 2017. As of August 6, 2018:
https://www.news.com.au/technology/innovation/hypervelocity-missile-breakthrough-makes-china-the-world-leader-in-new-weaponry/news-story/54cd94ab6883654575a028c1a6df6283

Shatz, Howard J., and Nathan Chandler, *Global Economic Trends and the Future of Warfare: The Changing Global Environment and Its Implications for the U.S. Air Force*, Santa Monica, Calif.: RAND Corporation, RR-2849/4, 2020. As of May 2020:
https://www.rand.org/pubs/research_reports/RR2849z4.html

Shinkman, Paul D., "Russia Has Deployed Thousands of Tanks, Troops to Ukraine, Top Official Says," *US News*, November 24, 2017. As of June 28, 2018:
https://www.usnews.com/news/world/articles/2017-11-24/russia-has-deployed-thousands-of-tanks-troops-to-ukraine-top-official-says

Shlapak, David A., and Michael Johnson, *Reinforcing Deterrence on NATO's Eastern Flank: Wargaming the Defense of the Baltics*, Santa Monica, Calif.: RAND Corporation, RR-1253-A, 2016. As of August 23, 2018:
https://www.rand.org/pubs/research_reports/RR1253.html

Shurkin, Michael, *The Abilities of the British, French, and German Armies to Generate and Sustain Armored Brigades in the Baltics*, Santa Monica, Calif.: RAND Corporation, RR-1629-A, 2017. As of August 24, 2018:
https://www.rand.org/pubs/research_reports/RR1629.html

Smith, Megan, and Sean M. Seigler, "Terrorism Before and After 911: A More Dangerous World?" *Research & Politics*, October–December 2017.

Sokolsky, Richard, The New NATO-Russia Military Balance: Implications for European Security, Washington, D.C.: Carnegie Endowment for World Peace, task force white paper, March 13, 2017. As of May 16, 2018:
http://carnegieendowment.org/2017/03/13/new-nato-russia-military-balance-implications-for-european-security-pub-68222

Speier, Richard H., George Narcouzi, Carrie Lee, and Richard M. Moore, *Hypersonic Missile Nonproliferation: Hindering the Spread of a New Class of Weapons*, Santa Monica, Calif.: RAND Corporation, RR-2137-CC, 2017. As of February 18, 2019:
https://www.rand.org/pubs/research_reports/RR2137.html

Starr, Barbara, "Pentagon: North Korean Special Forces 'Highly Trained, Well-Equipped,'" CNN, February 12, 2016. As of May 17, 2018:
https://www.cnn.com/2016/02/12/politics/pentagon-north-korean-special-forces-highly-trained-well-equipped/

Trevithick, Joseph, "SAMs and Anti-Ship Missiles Are Now Guarding China's South China Sea Islands," *The Drive*, May 3, 2018. As of June 28, 2018: http://www.thedrive.com/the-war-zone/20616/sams-and-anti-ship-missiles-are-now-guarding-chinas-man-made-south-china-sea-islands

Turing, A. M., "Computing Machinery and Intelligence," *Mind*, Vol. 59, No. 236, October 1950, pp. 433–460. As of May 27, 2018: https://academic.oup.com/mind/article/LIX/236/433/986238

U.S. Department of Defense, *Summary of the 2018 National Defense Strategy of the United States of America: Sharpening the American Military's Competitive Edge*, Washington, D.C., 2018. As of August 22, 2018: https://www.defense.gov/Portals/1/Documents/pubs/2018-National-Defense-Strategy-Summary.pdf

von Clausewitz, Carl, *On War*, ed. and trans., Michael Howard and Peter Paret, Princeton, N.J.: Princeton University Press, 1984.

Watts, Stephen, Bryan Frederick, Jennifer Kavanagh, Angela O'Mahoney, Thomas S. Szayna, Matthew Lane, Alexander Stephenson, and Colin P. Clarke, *A More Peaceful World? Regional Conflict Trends and U.S. Defense Planning*, Santa Monica, Calif.: RAND Corporation, RR-1177-A, 2017. As of February 18, 2019: https://www.rand.org/pubs/research_reports/RR1177.html

Weber, Max, "Politics as a Vocation," one of a series of lectures delivered to the Free Students Union, Munich, January 28, 1919. As of May 24, 2018: http://anthropos-lab.net/wp/wp-content/uploads/2011/12/Weber-Politics-as-a-Vocation.pdf

White House, *National Security Strategy of the United States of America*, Washington, D.C., December 2017.

Wood, L. Todd, "With U.S. Distracted, Russia Warms to Opportunities in 'Frozen Conflicts,'" *Washington Times*, April 20, 2017. As of May 23, 2018: https://www.washingtontimes.com/news/2017/apr/20/us-distracted-russia-warms-opportunities-frozen-co/

Work, Clint, "What Do Younger South Koreans Think of North Korea?" *The Diplomat*, February 2, 2018. As of May 21, 2018: https://thediplomat.com/2018/02/what-do-younger-south-koreans-think-of-north-korea/

Zakaria, Fareed, *The Future of Freedom: Illiberal Democracy at Home and Abroad*, New York: W. W. Norton, 2003.